WALKING IN THE COTSWOLDS

About the Author

Damian Hall is a freelance outdoor journalist who grew up in Nailsworth. He didn't think much to the Cotswolds when young because it didn't have any good football teams and Radiohead never played there. He travelled and lived abroad for seven years, trekked many of the world's famous and not so famous long-distance trails, fell down mountains in New Zealand's Southern Alps and had a walking boot stolen by a hungry possum in Australia. Yet when it was time to settle down Damian returned to the Cotswolds, where he now lives with his wife, daughter, a soft spot for Forest Green Rovers and a new walking boot.

The tea-loving hillbilly says the Cotswolds do something odd but pleasurable to him deep inside. Forced to pick a favourite spot, it would have to be Uley Bury's dramatic hillfort. He's a member of the Outdoor Writers and Photographers Guild, contributes regularly to *Country Walking* and *Outdoor Fitness* and also wrote the official guide to the Pennine Way.

Anyone interested in guided walks in the Cotswolds should get in touch via www.damianhall.info.

WALKING IN THE COTSWOLDS

by Damian Hall

2 POLICE SQUARE, MILNTHORPE, CUMBRIA LA7 7PY
www.cicerone.co.uk

© Damian Hall 2014
First edition 2014
ISBN: 978 1 85284 692 3

Printed in China on behalf of Latitude Press Ltd.
A catalogue record for this book is available from the British Library.
All photographs are by the author unless otherwise stated.

CW indicates a route which includes part of the Cotswold Way National Trail.

Advice to Readers

While every effort is made by our authors to ensure the accuracy of guidebooks as they go to print, changes can occur during the lifetime of an edition. If we know of any, there will be an Updates tab on this book's page on the Cicerone website (www.cicerone.co.uk), so please check before planning your trip. We also advise that you check information about such things as transport, accommodation and shops locally. Even rights of way can be altered over time. We are always grateful for information about any discrepancies between a guidebook and the facts on the ground, sent by email to info@cicerone.co.uk or by post to Cicerone, 2 Police Square, Milnthorpe LA7 7PY, United Kingdom.

Front cover: Walking along the edge of Rodborough Common towards Stroud on a crisp winter's morning

CONTENTS

Route symbols on OS map extracts
(for OS legend see printed OS maps)

〜〜〜   route

〜〜〜   alternative route

(🚶)   start/finish point

◀   route direction

Features on the overview map

———   County/Unitary boundary

        Urban area

        Area of Outstanding Natural
        Beauty eg *Wye Valley*

        400m
        200m
        75m
        0m

Acknowledgements

Huge, heartfelt thank-yous to Jenny Walters, Nick Hallissey, Rachel Broomhead and all at the continuously brilliant *Country Walking* (especially Editor Jonathan Manning), Jonathan Williams and all his team at Cicerone; Tom Bailey, Jon Sparks, Rudolf Abraham, Mark Bauer, Kev Reynolds, Tristan Gooley, Paul Tubb, John Burnett, Elizabeth Elliott, Mark Donald, Paul Simpson, Celso de Campos Jr, Vickie Bevan, Bevo, Jo, Kelvin, Barbara, Amy and Indy. And to the Cotswold Voluntary Wardens and everyone who helps maintain footpaths and keep the region such a wonderful place to tramp and live.

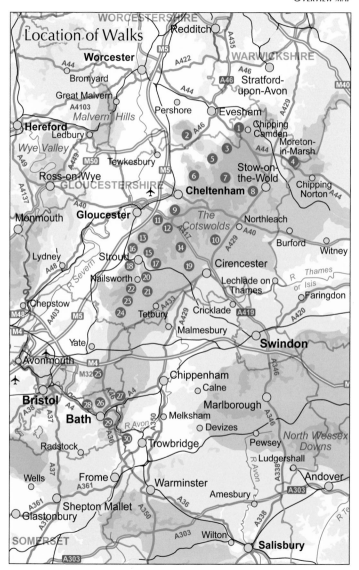

Aiming straight for Chipping Campden (Walk 1)

INTRODUCTION

Quintessential England... chocolate-box pretty... gentle, undulating hills... It's almost as if there's a law against describing the Cotswolds without using these clichés. But it's all hogwash. Well, okay, not completely. But from these lazy platitudes you might imagine the Cotswolds was a real-life Hobbiton: cosy, idyllic hills where everything's plump, prosperous and peaceful, and little has changed for hundreds of years. And, yes, there is some truth in that. But there's another side to the hardy hill chain that ripples and bulges all the way from Warwickshire and Worcestershire down through Gloucestershire to Somerset and Wiltshire, for some

145km (90 miles). In fact, covering 466km^2 (790 square miles), this is the second largest protected landscape in England, after the Lake District, and the largest Area of Outstanding Natural Beauty in England and Wales.

While it is true that the more seasoned hill-walker may see the Cotswolds as a soft touch, get to know these stout, gutsy, timeless hills and valleys and you'll find places of satisfying remoteness, authentic wildness and real drama. There are steep gradients to do battle with, 200-metre-plus climbs, while on the Edge, or on big, windy plateaus, the weather can treat you like you've insulted its mother.

Views along the bottom of the Edge over a drystone wall on the way down to Dyrham (Walk 25)

Coming downhill from the monument near Beckbury Camp (Walk 5)

After all, it was the Cotswolds that shaped adventurer and naturalist Dr Edward Wilson, who died a hero by Captain Robert Scott's side in a tent in Antarctica. One of Britain's most famous adventurers, David Hempleman-Adams, has lived here for many years. The Alfred Wainwright of the Cotswolds, *Cider With Rosie* author Laurie Lee (see Walk 15), hitchhiked to Spain aged 19 and took part in their Civil War. These are the sorts of people the region creates and attracts.

Indeed the evocative landscapes have long appealed to creative types too. The Cotswolds seduced esteemed artist, writer and Arts and Crafts Movement-mastermind William Morris, as well as poet WH Davies, author of the immortal line:

> *What is this life if, full of care,*
> *We have no time to stand and*
> *stare?*

Talking of wordsmiths, one William Shakespeare certainly didn't think the Cotswolds a soft touch. From *Richard II* come the lines:

> *I am a stranger here in*
> *Gloucestershire,*
> *These high wild hills and rough*
> *uneven ways*
> *Draws out our miles, and makes*
> *them wearisome*

The lush green hills and valleys were, however, much-loved by the invading Romans, the warring clans before them and the warring clans after them. And not to be left out, it's where Roundheads and Cavaliers fought some of the Civil War's bloodiest battles. So there's an awful lot about the region that isn't gentle and chocolate-box pretty.

The Cotswolds can be a place of stirring drama and the best place to experience that is on the Edge, the limestone escarpment with its biblical views stretching across the Vales of the Severn, Berkeley and Gloucester, and the River Severn (the country's longest), to JRR Tolkien's Forest of Dean, the jagged Malverns and the morose mountains of Wales. From below the scarp, on a frosty morning, the limestone Edge can resemble an Antarctic ice cliff; or in summer, a green tsunami halted, compellingly, mid-wave above you.

While there's an argument for the adventurousness of the Cotswolds being overlooked, these glorious limestone lumps also offer ideal walking territory for the less experienced hiker. The region is crisscrossed with around 4830km (3000 miles) of often well-waymarked public footpaths and so you can't get genuinely lost for long.

Away from the Edge, nowhere does valleys quite like the Cotswolds: teasingly clandestine, intimate and overgrown, but also sometimes deep, wide and long. Influential novelist JB Priestley visited the Cotswolds for 1933's travelogue *English Journey* and likened the region to a fairy tale and pleaded for it to be preserved. He recorded:

> Those green little valleys at once make you feel so oddly remote, miles and miles from anywhere, clean out of the world… you have only to take a turn or two from a main road, into one of these enchanted little valleys, these misty cups of verdure and

Climbing back out of the valley from Naunton (Walk 8)

11

grey walls, and you are gone and lost, somewhere at the end of space.

Elsewhere, the region's glorious beech woodlands, at times covering the steep escarpment, may have you dialling the fire brigade at first glance in autumn. Then there are those syrupy villages, drystone walls and centuries-old churches that seem to glow in the sunshine. There is mystery and history, too, in theatrically placed hillforts – there are 35 here – Roman ruins, enigmatic stone circles, Neolithic long barrows, round barrows, castles, shams, follies and stately homes full of strange stories. And claims of big cat sightings. There are also canals, many a nature reserve and Site of Special Scientific Interest, rare flowers (orchids especially), unusual bats and treasured butterflies. But best of all are those handsome hills, remote-feeling valleys and that glorious Edge.

GEOLOGY AND LANDSCAPE

The region's geography is defined by two things: limestone and a large, sloping plateau. The Cotswold hills may reach a comparatively modest 330m (1082ft), but they are a unique shape and part of the country's largest continuous geological feature. The gigantic slab of limestone stretches all the way from Dorset to Yorkshire, the Cotswolds being the most prominent part. Gradient builds gradually from the east in Oxfordshire, almost unnoticeably, even a little sneakily, until suddenly the floor plummets

Towards a former hillfort on Haresfield Beacon and some giant views south along the Edge and across the Severn Vale to Wales (Walk 16)

from beneath your feet at the western Edge, or scarp – to reveal vast views.

The oolitic limestone was formed in warm tropical seas 140–210 million years ago, in the Jurassic period. It's a compressed mishmash of sediments of clay, sand and the remains of billions of sea creatures. The stone is rich with fossils – look at a Cotswold cottage up close and you'll likely spy numerous crushed shells – and the first officially recognised dinosaur was found in the Cotswolds, at Stonesfield, in 1824. Unquarried, the rock can resemble tightly packed fish eggs, hence the name Oolite (from *òoion*, the Hellenic for egg) or 'egg stone'. Cleeve Common (Walk 6) and Leckhampton Hill (Walk 9) have the thickest sections of exposed Jurassic limestone anywhere in the country. Indeed some

of the most important research in the early days of geology was undertaken in the Cotswolds, so the area's strongly connected to the development of the subject – the theory of strata was developed near Bath.

Around the end of the last Ice Age, some 10,000 years ago, pressure from the ice cap caused the giant limestone slab to buckle, forming the Cotswolds. The melting snow and ice became rivers and streams, gradually cutting down through the limestone and giving the landscape those smooth contours. West of the Edge, 'outlier hills', such as Bredon Hill (see Walk 2) and Cam Long Down (see Walk 22) were once part of the scarp, but progressive erosion has banished them as cast-offs or outlaws, indicating where the Edge used to be.

Views across the green fields, hedges and woods of the Byzantine Box Valley (Walk 27)

The area from Stroud northeast to Chipping Campden is characterised as a broad, undulating, elevated plateau or 'high wold'. It is a windswept landscape that feels invigoratingly open, with big skies and deep valleys that sometimes can't be seen until you're upon them.

The north Cotswolds has been penetrated by large rivers, such as the Windrush, Coln, Leach and Evenlode, sculpting valleys. They all flow southeast to join the Thames – a Cotswold river too. Only around Stroud do the rivers flow westwards, the shortest way to the sea. The Avon forms a natural southern boundary to the Cotswolds, even if it has a will of its own, flowing east, then south, then west through Bradford-on-Avon and Bath.

Moving south-eastwards away from the high wold the landscape falls gently, a 'dip-slope' transition from plateau to lowland. Although this undulating landscape is still elevated, it feels more sheltered and intimate with fewer big views – here you'll find deep, dry valleys that can feel pleasingly secretive – before reaching the Cotswold lowlands, around Tetbury.

In the south Cotswolds, bigger valleys around Bath and Stroud, such as Swainswick (Walk 26), the Golden Valley (Walk 17) and Slad (Walk 15), were formed by a wider system of rivers.

Aside from those hardy folk in the Iron Age, who preferred the hilltops, most settlements have sprung up below the scarp or in valleys and 'combes' (meaning hollow or fold). Indeed many places have taken their name from the landscape, such as Edge, Wotton-under-Edge and Sheepscombe (wonderfully combining the natural surroundings with the region's traditional industry). Yet considering how many people live in the Cotswolds, it should be much, much uglier. But the oolitic stone, used to build most of the cottages, villages, drystone walls, churches and manor houses, gives the region a pleasing uniformity. The limestone has been an obvious natural resource for locals to build their homes, long barrows and more since the Bronze Age (2000–650BC). As well as there being lots of it, the stone is comparatively easy to shape when fresh from the ground, but hardens over time. The uniformity of stone often masks the fact that houses can be hundreds of years older or newer than their neighbours yet you'd hardly know it.

And, of course, there's the colour – the Cotswolds have their own aesthetic. Oolitic limestone has a special, lingering glow in sunlight, especially at dusk. Often likened to honey or syrup, the stone seems to absorb sunlight, preserving and magnifying its warm colour. 'As if they know the trick of keeping the lost sunlight of centuries glimmering about them', wrote JB Priestley. 'This lovely trick is at the very heart of the Cotswold mystery.' The stone's colour varies across the region, tending to be more honey-golden and buttery in the north, a little greyer or more silvery and creamier in the south.

Because the stone on top of the land is often the same stone a few feet below it, from a distance many of these man-made structures seem to merge right into the natural landscape. For once, man and nature close to being in some kind of harmony – and a beguiling one at that.

Almost everything about the Cotswolds – its shape, the soil, plants and animals, man's industry, culture and history – is directly linked to the golden stone under these hills.

PLANTS AND WILDLIFE

Although the Cotswolds landscape has been farmed and managed for centuries, there's still plenty that's wild and natural to take joy in. From the omnipresent limestone many green things have grown and the Cotswolds Area of Outstanding Natural Beauty (AONB) was designated in recognition of its 'rich, diverse and high quality landscape'.

As well as five European Special Areas of Conservation, three National Nature Reserves and over 80 Sites of Special Scientific Interest, the region has over 50 per cent of the country's Jurassic 'unimproved' grassland, meaning it's been relatively untampered with by farming down the ages, probably because the top soil is thin.

Cleeve Common is perhaps the best example of ancient limestone grasslands, with around 150 species of herb and grass, plus rainbows of rare wild flowers in summer and the equally precious

Ragwort on the wonderfully named Nibley Knoll, a geological Site of Special Scientific Interest, with the Tyndale Monument behind (Walk 24)

Pretty scabious line the route towards Shenberrow Hill (Walk 3)

butterflies they attract. But Selsley (Walk 18), Haresfield (Walk 16), Minchinhampton, Rodborough Commons (both Walk 20) and Crickley Hill (Walk 9), to mention a few, offer similar natural treasures.

The most notable species of orchids to be found are green-winged and early purple (late April and May), common spotted, pyramid, musk, bee and frog (summer). Many other rare species thrive in this seemingly nutrient poor soil, such as the rare and beautiful pasque flower (purple and gold) and Cotswold pennycress. Elsewhere, you'll likely see white oxeye daises, bird's-foot trefoil, scabious, kidney vetch (which attract the common blue, the rare chalkhill blue and Duke of Bergundy butterflies), thyme, salad burnet, hoary plantain, rock-rose and knapweeds. You could also see wild roses, wood anemones, harebells and cowslips in meadows, plus honeysuckle adds a sweet fragrance in spring. Snowdrops and hawthorn bushes add splashes of white, as do some hedgerows – which can be ancient too – when interwoven with old man's beard.

Much of the woodland cover is ancient and tree vegetation tends to change as you climb the escarpment, from ash, sycamore and scrub lower down to beech higher up, the Cotswolds signature tree. Due to its thick canopy and carpet of leaf litter it's not a tree that helps other species thrive underneath, but no one's complaining in autumn when they make the Cotswolds look like they're on fire (for more tree worship, visit the National Arboretum at Westonbirt near Tetbury; www.forestry.gov.uk/westonbirt). There's a good deal of hazel and oak about too, and beautiful silver birch. Much of the woodland along the scarp is ancient and among the most diverse and species-rich of its type.

In woods below the scarp, you'll find green carpets of dog's mercury (February to April), then spreads of bluebells (April to June), with their wafting natural perfume. In fact the UK has half the world's bluebell population, which are often an indicator of ancient woodland. They start flowering in the southwest before fanning out across the country. Around the same time, the unmistakable smell of wild garlic (ramsons) adds plenty of aroma. In farmland in spring and summer you may see the vivid clash of bright red poppies and the brilliant yellow oil rapeseed (fast becoming a tourist attraction in their own right). You'll also likely see the thistle-esque teasel, which has a special historical place in the Cotswolds. The spiky heads were used in the manufacture of cloth, to raise the nap (the fuzzy surface on velvet).

When it comes to the wild things, woodpeckers keep the techno-folk music going while the chiffchaff is another woodland dweller. Kingfishers rule the roost along riverbanks, while buzzards (listen for a distinctive mewing call), kestrels and sparrowhawks

Crocuses on a wooded path near Bisley (Walk 17)

hover up high, like a merciless secret police. The puff-chested meadow pipit (oft confused with the skylark) is perhaps the Cotswolds signature bird, while bullfinches and yellowhammers dart between hawthorn and gorse. Dippers and grey wagtails (near fast-running streams), mandarins (woodlands), corn buntings and willow tits can all be seen. Migrating ring ouzels and wheaters stop off in spring (look on open hills and golf courses), while chaffinches, skylarks and meadow pipits call by in autumn. In winter look for black-headed and common gulls. Alarmist pheasants seem to be everywhere.

Deer sightings are possible, while foxes, badgers, rabbits, hares and grey squirrels could well be glimpsed. Look for dormice in hazel coppices and some very rare bats in caves between Minchinhampton and Nailsworth. Also keep an eye out for big wild cats – some locals swear there's one, or maybe more, about.

THE IMPACT OF MAN

The first Cotswolders were Mesolithic nomads who hunted and gathered in a heavily wooded region 10,000 years ago. In around 4000BC Neolithic man cut down many of the trees, for crop farming, but they left us their long barrows – huge mysterious tombs, such as Belas Knap (Walk 6) and Nympsfield Long Barrow (Walk 18).

The Bronze Age (2000–650BC) saw a more nomadic way of life, although they left round barrows and stone circles, such as at Rollright (Walk 4). The Iron Age (800BC to Roman occupation) saw waves of Celtic tribes invade and some 35 hillforts built. Rather than military strongholds, they were designed to be visible and were built in prominent positions along the Edge, such as at Uley Bury (Walk 22), Painswick Beacon (Walks 11 and 13), Cleeve Common (Walk 6) and Crickley Hill (Walk 9). Strip lynchets, a series of farming terraces, can also be seen in the Cotswolds and date from between the Bronze Age and early medieval period.

What did the Romans do for us? Arriving in AD43 they built Cirencester, Gloucester and Bath, plus lavish, mosaic-floored villas, such

Belas Knap is a particularly good example of a Neolithic long barrow, featuring a false entrance; theories differ as to why (Walk 6)

as Chedworth (Walk 10) and Great Witcombe (Walk 11). Cirencester, or rather Corinium, was the second largest city in Britain and a centre of a new trade: wool. The Romans discovered that the well-drained hills provided excellent pasture and started large-scale sheep farming.

Next came the Saxons, from Germany, and the Dark Ages. There was a major battle on Hinton Hill (Walk 25) where the Saxons beat the Britons, and little Winchcombe (Walks 5 and 6) became the capital of the Saxon kingdom of Mercia. It's likely the phrase 'Cot's Wold' comes from the Anglo-Saxon period. Sheep were grazed in large 'cots' or enclosures on the wolds, originally in Cutsdean in the north Cotswolds. A literal translation of Cotswolds is 'sheep-hills' and a direct contemporary German translation means 'high

wooded land' (the hilltops were more wooded then). Semi-plausible and mildly chortlesome theories of chieftains and gods named Cot or Cod abound too.

The Normans arrived in 1066 briefly making Gloucester the country's capital and bringing another era of prosperity to the region. They built churches and carried out their landmark Domesday Book survey, recording that the area was heavily cultivated but the west was very wooded (and that there was only one wall!). The Romans started the wool trade, but the Normans moved it up a level. More land was cleared for grazing and sheep soon outnumbered people four to one, while the church pretty much ran the industry. The Cotswold Lion breed – big, hornless with a white face and long heavy fleece – became prized for its excellence (their

Many Cotswold churches were built with wool money, but Painswick's (Walk 13) may pre-date the Normans

descents can be seen at the Cotswold Farm Park, near Walk 7).

By the Middle Ages the Cotswolds was one big grazing pasture and wool exports accounted for more than half England's wealth – half of that came from this region. A wealthy new middle class was created and their money was often ploughed into building manor houses and 'wool churches', such as in Chipping Campden and Winchcombe. Many of the Cotswolds' best-looking buildings come from this period of prosperity.

The second half of the 15th century brought a decline to the wool trade, from high taxes and competition from Spain. But a cloth industry emerged, started by home manufacturers, especially in the Five Valleys around Stroud, which soon teemed with 150 water-powered mills. They produced the Stroudwater Scarlet and Uley Blue, from natural river salts that gave vivid and long-lasting colour for military uniforms.

The English Civil Wars of the 17th century saw several significant battles in the Cotswolds as the area had strategic importance. The bloody Battle of Lansdown (Walk 26) took place near Bath, where the scarped landscape played a key part, and the churches in Painswick and Winchcombe still bear Civil War scars.

Between 1700 and 1840 large tracts of the Cotswolds were cordoned off as private land by the Enclosures Act, the biggest change to the region in centuries. It was a land grab by the rich, depriving local people of their rights to graze animals and collect wood on common land, creating Britain's working class in the process. The Act brought the region most of its drystone walls, often as boundary markers – although the art dated back to the Stone Age, appropriately, when the same style was used for long barrows. Today the 6000km of walls are roughly equivalent in length to the Great Wall of China.

The cloth mills were eventually out-manoeuvred by their Yorkshire rivals, who could move their product on quicker thanks to coal and steam-power, and from the 1850s a long period of poverty ensued that, ironically, ensured an economic future for the Cotswolds as a tourist destination. The lack of coal meant industrial overdevelopment didn't arrive and the economic downturn helped keep the Cotswolds looking as good as they do today. Old mills have been attractively renovated and abandoned canals have become wildlife havens.

In the 1890s William Morris and his followers established the Cotswolds, initially Chipping Campden, as a thriving centre for the Arts and Crafts Movement (their buildings can be seen in Campden, Painswick and Sapperton), an antidote to Industrialisation, which included an implicit call for a return to nature. Writers and artists followed, foreshadowing the 21st-century flock of tiresome, phone-hacked celebrities. And Morris was also very active in preserving older buildings, especially churches. During World War I open wolds were ploughed for extra food and woods were scavenged for timber, while World War II saw numerous airfields built atop the plateaus (see Walk 10).

Today some four-fifths of the Cotswolds is agricultural land. But there are still sheep about, some quarries are still in use and even two mills (see Walk 17) are still going. Tourism is the biggest industry now, bringing in around a billion pounds annually. Happily, however, traditional skills – from potters to textile designers and glassmakers to blacksmiths and silversmiths – still prosper too. Put simply,

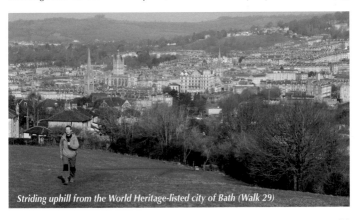

Striding uphill from the World Heritage-listed city of Bath (Walk 29)

it is unlikely anywhere that's had this much history looks this good.

WHEN TO VISIT

You can visit the Cotswolds any time, although summer does get busy, more so in the northern end and Bath, but there are quieter walks in this book for that very time. Autumn sets those beech woodlands ablaze; in fact because of its unique topography, autumn can come a month early to the Edge. While down in the Vale late-summer flowers are still blooming, trees 300m above them have turned red, orange and yellow. Winter can be wonderful, with the woods denuded and the views bigger, while prices drop and trails are deliciously crisp and quiet. When the snowdrops have left, spring sees the place awash with daffodils and the bleat of lambs.

GETTING AROUND

Bath, Stroud, Cam and Dursley, Gloucester, Cheltenham and Moreton-on-the-Marsh all have train stations and, possibly with some minimal bus catching involved, provide useful bases for several of the walks in this book. With your own wheels, Painswick, Nailsworth and Winchcombe are more enticing options; smaller and quieter, with more of a classic Cotswold feel and scenic settings. And there's World Heritage-listed Bath of course. For what it's worth, Winchcombe, Stroud, King's Stanley and Leonard Stanley, and Bradford-on-Avon are all official 'walker friendly towns', meaning the local council has paid greater attention to maintaining footpaths and facilities for walkers.

In truth, public transport options for long journeys across the Cotswolds can be frustrating, so if you're planning a long weekend of walking it makes

Box Woods gloriously aflame on a sunny autumn day (Walk 27)

more sense to have one base and explore that area thoroughly rather than try and cover off both ends of the hill chain. For transport, the Department of Transport's TransportDirect.info (which also offers car journey info) and TraveLine.info are good transport search engines, while the AA Route Planner is good for car journeys (www.theaa.com/route-planner).

WHERE TO STAY

The Cotswolds have something of a north–south divide. With the Chipping Campdens, Broadways and Bourton-on-the-Waters, the north tends to attract bigger tourist crowds. So for a quieter time during sunnier months, you're better off heading south (ignoring Bath too, of course).

The Cotswolds is a major tourist destination so it's eminently well set-up for accommodation, from luxury B&Bs and boutique hotels (from £50 a night) to self-catering cottages (from around £250 a week) and family run campsites (from £5 a person); many village pubs also offer B&B. Sadly there are no hostels particularly well located for these walks (but Stow-on-the-Wold's might prove useful). For accommodation a good first port of call is the official tourism website (www.cotswolds.com), but the excellent *Rough Guide to the Cotswolds* guidebook may give more considered tips. Local tourist offices can be useful for researching and booking accommodation too. Contact details of a selection of these are given in Appendix D.

Book well ahead if you intend to visit in summer. As you'd expect with all those farms, the Cotswolds have plenty of great culinary options, and lots of very fine pubs serving real ales and local ciders.

Spacious, sun-kissed woods in Ashcombe Bottom (Walk 14)

TERRAIN AND WHAT TO TAKE

Terrain includes fields, woodland paths (likely to be muddy), old drove-roads, green lanes, farm tracks and occasional minor roads. I've tried to keep routes off tarmac whenever possible but sometimes a quiet country lane beckons, or a scamper across something busier is worth it to get to somewhere grand.

Because of the tragicomic nature of British weather, it's always worth carrying a waterproof jacket, an extra layer (it can be windy on the Edge especially – and from where, as most British weather comes from the south west, you can often see it charging at you like a cavalry of apocalyptic horsemen), water, a snack and a mobile phone.

MAPS

The routes described in this guide are only suggestions. Do go off piste, explore on a whim, follow a disappearing deer's tail into woods or the vague promise of wildflowers on distant grasslands.

But if you are going freestyle take a map. The maps used here are Landranger, with a scale of 1:50,000, used because they fit the book format better. The Explorer map, with a scale of 1:25,000 shows more detail, and so is the better purchase for walkers. But if you're sticking to this book's suggested routes you should be fine with the maps here. You can't go wrong for long in the Cotswolds. It's not Alaska. You'll meet a road soon enough, and tarmac leads to cars and houses.

14 walks in this book follow parts of the Cotswold Way National Trail, which is well waymarked, often with the acorn symbol

Views at dusk along Stinchbome Hill towards the Tyndale Monument and Wotton-under-Edge (Walk 22)

USING THIS GUIDE

The 30 walks here aren't historical walks, or pub or café walks, or (perhaps with the exception of Walk 8) walks specifically designed to include the most picturesque villages. These are simply the 30 best walks in the Cotswolds, according to this humble local. But almost always they do include some of the above. For the biblical views, the most rewarding walking is done along, or very close to, the Edge so most walks include a section of it and there's usually a climb involved to get there.

Fourteen of the walks here include parts of the brilliant Cotswold Way National Trail (CW) that snakes for 164km (102 miles) from Chipping Campden to Bath, mostly hugging the limestone scarp (look for the acorn symbol). These walks are indicated on the contents page with this symbol: **CW**. If you walked all 14 you'd have covered about two-thirds of the trail and certainly its finest sections. When a walk in this guidebook strays from the Edge, you'll know there's a special reason for it.

All the walks are circular and are estimated to take from three to six hours, although time estimates are only very loose approximations (very roughly, on average most people cover around 4km an hour). Extra time should be allowed for the many breaks you will want to take. The longer walks usually have suggested shortcuts, while the shorter walks often have ideas for extensions. The routes have been graded from 1 to 3. A 1 would be around three hours and without much gradient. A 3 would be longer and more strenuous. A long

Looking towards Cam Long Down from Coaley Peak (Walk 18)

walk without much gradient might be a 2. As terrain and navigation doesn't vary greatly, these grades are more about fitness levels.

Signage is generally good, especially when following an established long-distance path. (National Trails, like the Cotswold Way, are often marked with a simple silhouette of an acorn.) I've tried to be detailed with the route description where it might need concentration, for example through woods or a series of fields. But where things are straightforward I haven't mentioned every stile and gate. You don't want to spend a whole walk with your head in this book.

Lastly, the Cotswolds has plenty of independent shops, cafés and pubs: where possible please keep the local economy going and opt for these rather than multinationals.

WALK 1

*Chipping Campden, Broadway
and Broadway Tower*

Start/Finish	Market Hall, Chipping Campden (SP 153 393)
Distance	18km (11 miles)
Grade	2
Time	5hrs
Maps	OS Landranger 151 and 150 or Explorer OL45
Refreshments	Pubs and cafés in Chipping Campden and Broadway; café at Broadway Tower
Public transport	Buses from Evesham and Stow-on-the-Wold
Parking	Along the main street in Chipping Campden, or at Dover's Hill

This one's a belter. Two of the north Cotswolds' A-list short walks are so close you may as well stick them together to be enjoyed in one merry gambol. From famously handsome Chipping Campden, follow the Cotswold Way up to Dover's Hill and across fields to sugar-sweet Broadway. Take a testing climb to Broadway Tower, the second highest point in the Cotswolds and one of the finest viewpoints in England. Then it's back to Campden on the Cotswold Way via pleasant fields and a peaceful, wide avenue. Both Broadway and Campden are tourist honeypots so, if possible, save this walk for less sunny months.

Starting where the **Cotswold Way** (CW) also begins, by the Market Hall, head past the war memorial and west-south-west along the high street. Turn right, by the church and when the road bends right leave it to the left (the second exit) on a lane past some lovely thatched cottages. ▶

The lane becomes a track and ascends steeply – look for Broadway Tower, your objective, away to the left. At the road turn left for about 50 metres then right at a CW sign, between hawthorn hedges. Go through a gate, turn left and head towards the **Dover's Hill** trig point. You may well feel you haven't yet earned a view this good.

Trace the Edge left/south and after a topograph leave the CW to head right and downhill. Look for a

The first of these cottages belonged to novelist Graham Greene.

27

CHIPPING CAMPDEN, DOVER'S HILL AND THE COTSWOLD OLIMPICKS

A bench to enjoy the big views across the Vale of Evesham from Dover's Hill, site of the Cotswold Olimpicks

Chipping Campden might be Cotswold's most elegant town, but it's no secret. Parts of the high street date to the 14th century while the signature Market Hall is 17th century, when wool was sold at the market then sent straight to Italy and the Low Countries via Southampton. 'Chipping' means 'market' (via the word 'cheap') in Olde English, while Campden meant 'cultivated valley' to the Saxons.

Early last century the town was the centre of the William Morris-led Arts and Crafts Movement – an antithesis to Industrialisation – and writers and artist settled here. Today's Campden is still a hot bed for arts and crafts – and morris dancing.

The Cotswold Olimpick Games take place on the Friday after Spring Bank Holiday, on nearby Dover's Hill. Started in 1612 by local lawyer Robert Dover, competitions include welly wanging and shin kicking, and there's a torchlight procession. Now National Trust-owned, there was a Civil War battle here and it's said you can see for 96km (60 miles).

walkers' gate on the left (before the bigger farm gate). Turn right onto the lane and downhill. Turn left over a stile into fields. At a wooden animal shelter bear right and go through a kissing-gate to descend through the middle of a field to a double stile. Then follow a fence to another stile and continue down through fields. Cross a track by houses and go past a magnificent oak tree on your right.

After crossing a stream you reach a junction of several paths. Take the second option on your left (Buckle Lane) that leads through woodland to a lane. Turn left and uphill for about half a kilometre to a road junction. Here, turn right, then take the bridleway on the left. Cross the edge of a golf course on your way to the busy **A44**, which you duck under. Turn left down a lane, then right to join the main street through winsome **Broadway**.

> Worcestershire's **Broadway** is another pleasing Cotswold cliché: flanked with red-flowered chestnut trees and with wisteria-clothed cottages built with probably the yellowest limestone you ever did see. The settlement probably dates back to the Romans but its heyday was as a stop-off on the coach route – note those wide streets and village name – from London to Worcester and several buildings date to the 17th century, while St Eadburgha's church dates to the 12th century. Many famous writers have lived here including Edward Elgar, *Peter Pan*-author JM Barrie, and Laura Ashley. Like Campden, it's brimming with teashops and postcards and gets too busy for some tastes.

At a road junction follow the sign for Snowshill. After a church on your left, turn left down a narrow lane that leads into a footpath. Then turn right in front of a bowls club. After about 100 metres turn left. Continue straight ahead, ignoring paths to the right and left, eventually joining the **Cotswold Way**. Follow yellow markers on wooden posts through several fields and directly uphill, through Broadway Coppice, which has coppiced hazel, oak, birch and ash, all the way up to **Broadway Tower**.

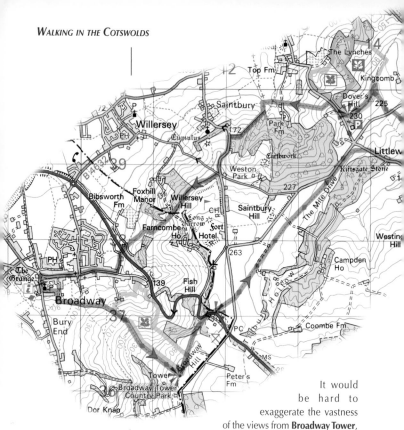

It would be hard to exaggerate the vastness of the views from **Broadway Tower**, a fine folly built on the second highest point in the Cotswolds (after Cleeve Common). It's said you can peer into 16 counties in a 62-mile radius from here. Completed in 1798, members of the Arts and Crafts Movement used the Tower as a holiday retreat – Pre-Raphaelite artists William Morris, Dante Gabriel Rossetti and Edward Burne-Jones were frequent visitors. The vantage point was also used to track enemy planes during the World Wars. More comfortably, nowadays there's a dog-friendly café, shop, museum and lots of stairs to climb to the top. **www.broadwaytower.co.uk**

From the Tower, turn north and follow CW way-markers back towards the A44. The curious lumps here are both Anglo-Saxon burial ground and the tomfoolery of modern machinery, although it can be a sea of wildflowers in summer. You're only in the woods, which smell of wild garlic, for a few minutes and it's well signposted.

Broadway Tower up close, where William Morris and other artists used to come for inspiration

31

At the A44 cross with care and go straight over into the trees (rather than following the CW right to a picnic area – there are public toilets here). Turn right and after a topograph turn left into a field full of pretty little white flowers in summer – almost like snowfall. Cross a road then continue through two fields, to the broad **Mile Drive**.

Follow this pleasing, grassy avenue for some time to a road. But just before the road take a right into a field (signposted CW), on a path running parallel to the tarmac. Near the end of the field duck downhill and right, directly towards **Chipping Campden**. Turn right onto the road. Turn left, off it, by a public footpath sign, through a field, then a pedestrian path that deposits you near the **church**.

WALK 2
Bredon Hill

Start/Finish	By church, Overbury (SO 958 374)
Distance	15km (9 miles); shorter versions 7.5km (4.5 miles)
Grade	3
Time	4hrs; shorter versions 2hrs
Maps	OS Landranger 150 or Explorer 205
Refreshments	Crown Inn, Kemerton; Star Inn, Ashton under Hill; Yew Tree, Conderton
Public transport	Buses from Cheltenham (Royal Well bus station)
Parking	By church

Bredon Hill should be much busier with walking boots than it is. The monster of a hill is an outlier, cast adrift from the Cotswold escarpment. For once in the Cotswolds you get the novel feeling of traditional hillwalking – and some sensational views to boot, plus hillfort remains. There's a fair bit of field walking, navigation is pretty good, ascents and descents are fairly gradual, and the route includes part of the Wychavon Way. Look out for yellowhammers, buzzards and fallow deer.

Park by **Overbury church** (with its 15th-century tower and Norman nave) and walk back out to the main road, turning right, towards Kemerton. Leave the pavement to the right through a metal kissing-gate by an old wooden signpost, and directly across a pasture field to a gate.

Follow the hedge to a small wooden gate and continue following hedge/fence to a metal kissing-gate. Reaching **Kemerton**, cross the road and angle slightly left to continue in the same direction. Turn right at a road junction and past a cemetery. As the road bends right leave it on a stony track going directly uphill. Great views open up – the Malverns and Cotswolds snaking south, the Vale of Evesham and Black Mountains on a clear day.

Look for a yellow arrow on a fence post to turn left between two hedges before a farm gate. Turn right over a wooden stile by a yellow waymarker and uphill. Go over a stile to the left and swing right to carry on in the same

direction through trees. Go over a stile into a field and straight on. At a **standing stone** angle right, with trees on your left, towards Sundial Farm.

Go through a wooden farm gate and onto a grassy track. Just before a building, leave the track to the left, over a stile. Follow the left edge of the field and a wall. Go over a stile and turn right.

Continue on an obvious path as it goes through trees then follow a wall as big views open up to the left. Go through a gate and you can see **Bradbury Stone Tower** and some earthworks. The path sticks to the wall, but you'll probably want to detour to the Tower.

Millions of years of erosion cast the 293m **Bredon Hill** adrift of the Cotswold Edge. The earthworks at the summit are the remains of Iron Age hillfort Kemerton Camp, probably abandoned in the first century AD after a big battle (the slashed remains of 50 bodies were discovered). There are also Roman earthworks and ancient standing stones here. The Banbury Stone is nicknamed 'Elephant Stone' for obvious reasons, while two stones near the summit are called the King and Queen Stones and it was believed passing between them would cure illness. The summit's chunky tower is called Parsons Folly and was built in the mid-18th century as a summer house. Bredon Hill features in plenty of poetry, writings and art, most famously in AE Housman's poem 21 from *A Shropshire Lad*:

Getting to the top of Bredon Hill is a bit of a slog, but well worth it

> *In summertime on Bredon*
> *The bells they sound so clear*
> *Round both the shires they ring them*
> *In steeples far and near*
> *A happy noise to hear.*

35

Even on cloudy days, the Malverns are clearly visible from the summit of Bredon Hill

Follow the wall as it swings east, along the top of the hill. Go through a big wooden gate by a walled copse – you're now on the **Wychavon Way** (WW). When the path divides take a right to follow the fence downhill through a metal gate and by the side of beech woodlands.

If you're taking one of the two shorter routes back to Overbury, turn right here.

Come to a crossroads of paths. ◄ Carry straight on and shortly come to another crossroads where, again, you continue on the same path. ◄ Follow the drystone wall for some time, until you start to go downhill and to the right. Leave the hilltop through a big wooden gate on the left, waymarked WW. Go through hawthorn trees and cross another track to continue downhill. Go through a metal gate. After the plateau of Little Hill look for a stile then wooden waymarkers to take you to **Ashton under Hill**.

If opting for the second shortcut, turn right for Overbury.

Go left by the **churchyard** wall to a wooden gate. If not detouring into the delightful village (with a **pub**), turn right before the gate and follow the bottom edge of the field by the fence, to a metal gate. Pass through it and diagonally right to another gate in the top corner of the field. Cross a track and take the path between two hedges then stick to the right of a field. Cross a foot-

bridge and continue across the next field, to a gate and onto a lane.

Walk on the tarmac for about 400 metres, then turn right by Middle Farm, and through sleepy **Grafton** to the lane's end. Look for a signpost to Conderton and go through a gate to bear half-right across a field to a fenced copse. Just after a standing stone, head diagonally right towards the top corner of the field and a stile by a wall.

Pass by the Overbury Estate's unfriendly sign and continue in a similar direction, skirting a hill to its right and towards a metal kissing-gate. Keep to the left of another unfriendly sign and into the next field. Go uphill and aim for the top left-hand corner by a building. Go through the little gate and turn right onto a grassy track going uphill. Go left at a junction and straight over at a crossroads.

The track bends to left before joining a lane, where you turn right. The lane goes downhill, then turn left at a junction into a pretty little road. Take a right near the bottom of the hill, when you see the church tower, to bring you back to the start.

On the way back down the north face of the Cotswolds can be seen

WALK 3

Stanton, Stanway and Snowshill

Start/Finish	Stanton Village Club car park, Stanton (SP 068 343)
Distance	13km (8 miles)
Grade	3
Time	5hrs
Maps	OS Landranger 150 or Explorer OL45
Refreshments	Mount Inn, Stanton; Snowshill Arms, Snowshill
Public transport	Buses from Cheltenham (Royal Wells Bus Station)

Some may vote this the best walk in the Cotswolds. It has stout hills, big views, history, arresting architecture and classically cute Cotswold villages – even those not particularly fussed about villages will have their heads turned, with at least two enchanting examples. Includes parts of the Cotswold and Winchcombe Ways, which aid navigation.

Stanton: the fairest of all Cotswold villages

Forget your mirror-obsessing Chipping Campdens, **Stanton** is the fairest of all Cotswold villages. The cottages seem the syrupyest, the flowers overhanging garden fences the biggest and brightest. The gorgeous, quiet, largely 16th-century-built village

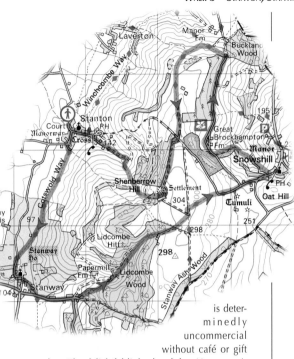

is deter-
minedly
uncommercial
without café or gift
shop. The delightful little church has Norman origins, a 15th-century tower and stained-glass windows from Hailes Abbey. Look for Stott lanterns,
a medieval cross in the middle of the village and
spectacular gargoyles on the church. Stanton means
'stony farm'.

You may not want to leave Stanton, of course, but if
you are still game for a stroll, turn right out of the car
park then right again at a T-junction, towards Stanway.
Continue through the village to a Stott lantern on the
left. Ignore the lane to the left and follow a **Cotswold
Way** (CW) signpost just beyond it, towards a farm, and
right, into pasture fields. Follow CW waymarkers through
several pretty fields with some magnificent trees – oaks,

chestnuts and especially a magnificent copper beech – and pleasing views to the right. At a lane, opposite a cricket field, turn left into **Stanway**.

> 'Stanway' is a reference to the old Salt Way trading route. The cricket field was donated by *Peter Pan*-author JM Barrie (1860-1937) who fell in love with Stanway and especially Stanway House where he holidayed repeatedly, entertaining the likes of Sir Arthur Conan Doyle and HG Wells. The Jacobean facade of 17th-century Stanway House is an arresting sight (limited opening times; **www.stanway-fountain.co.uk**) and behind it are spectacular water gardens including Britain's highest jet fountain (91m). Look for entertaining carved heads on the 12th-century church.

Continue on the road, past the **church** and **Stanway House**, turning left by a CW signpost and past an old gatehouse, a blacksmith's workshop and Stanway Water Mill on the right, looking for a swan head carved onto the next gate as you enter an orchard.

At the road turn left on the pavement and follow it for nearly half a kilometre, ignoring a CW signpost on the other side of the road. ◄ When the road bends a sharp right, leave it, heading straight on, by cottages. There's soon a fork – go straight up, following a sign to Snowshill and Stanton, while girding those loins for the day's steepest and longest climb.

This part of the CW is covered in Walk 5.

In **Lidcombe Wood**, after a small clearing take the right and more distinctive path at a fork and ignore two more right turns after it (if in doubt anywhere stick with most prominent track). The path bends right near the top and through thicker woodland, crosses another track then chucks you out for a rest at the top near a gate. Turn left (ignore a sharp left) and trace the edge of the woodland.

Go left at a path junction by a blue waymarker and through two arable fields. Bear left for about 50 metres then go right to follow a Winchcombe Way sign, which takes you diagonally across an arable field, through a gap

in a wall, through another field to a lane, and downhill into Snowshill. This route doesn't go into Snowshill itself, but you'd be foolhardy not to investigate – then walk back out to Oat House.

Snowshill: clinging to the top of the slope like a stubborn glacier

Snowshill is another adorable village, with its tasteful little Victorian church and semi-permanent bookstall on the village green. The village was seen on the big screen in 2001's *Bridget Jones's Diary*. The National Trust's nearby Snowshill Manor is a Tudor building with pretty terraced gardens and an extraordinary collection of 22,000 wonderful curios, from toys to bicycles and Samurai armour and stories of eccentric previous owner Charles Paget Wade, who liked to open the door to visitors wearing fancy dress.

Follow a paved track downhill opposite Oat House (on the right when you came into Snowshill initially). By a private property gate and pond go left on a narrow footpath following the hedge, then through a stile and gate and a few fields and up again towards **Great**

Brockhampton Farm. Aim to its left initially, then turn right onto a track and take the left at the fork. Follow this track for a while, looking back for views of Snowshill and Broadway Tower, also to the right.

Just after the track reaches a farm gate at the end of the woodland, take a left, off the track, at a walkers' gate. Go across the field, angling downhill, with views of the Vale of Evesham, Broadway and more. At a stile turn left to re-join the CW on a track. The CW, which you'll follow all the way back to Stanton, continues on a track by a fence, climbing up to the top of the edge again, on its limestone bedrock. Follow a farm track for some time.

When the track reaches a metalled track, follow CW signs over a cattle grid and right (not the first right), past a farmhouse and look for CW signs to take you downhill into a tree-lined gully (rather than the track to right), where you'll be accompanied by gorse and hawthorn. Around here, near the top of **Shenberrow Hill**, are the remains of a 1ha Iron Age settlement excavated in 1935 (pottery, a bronze bracelet and bone needles were found).

Follow a path through a pasture field (keep to right) to a stile to the right, in trees. After a pond, turn left onto a metalled farm track, which takes you back into the village and past a gorgeous thatched cottage. Turn left by a Stott lantern (not the one from earlier) and you should soon recognise where you are. Alternatively, turn right to find the Mount Inn and a well-earned drink.

WALK 4
Long Compton and the Rollright Stones

Start/Finish	Church, Long Compton (SP 287 331)
Distance	14km (9 miles); shorter version 11km (7 miles); plus 1km detour to Stones
Grade	2
Time	4.5hrs; shorter version 4hrs; plus 30min detour to Stones
Maps	OS Landranger 151 or Explorer 191
Refreshments	None
Public transport	Buses from Chipping Norton (Shipston Road)
Parking	Park on a lane near the church

This walk may not have the instant charm of some others – valleys are broader than classic Cotswold V-shapes here. But it has an agreeable character of its own, and the Cotswolds' most impressive stone circle, a place of mystery and legend. There's plenty of field walking and one sustained climb. But there are good views and navigation is mostly easy. The route follows part of the d'Arcy Dalton Way and, briefly, Shakespeare's Way.

From the **church**, with its curious house on top of a gate arrangement, head south on the **A3400** (main road) and take the second left, after the local shop ('Stores'). When the road swings right continue ahead onto a broad farm-track between fields going gradually uphill.

The track kinks left then straightens to go through farm buildings. After a short climb the track goes into a new field and swings sharply left/uphill – here take a right into a field and downhill by an old sign that's hard to spot.

Go over a footbridge at the valley bottom and follow the edge of a field, then turn left to go uphill in the same field. From here it's a slow climb up the other side of the valley, mostly following field edges, to find the road near Great Rollright.

The only point of possible confusion is: near the top, after two gates close together, go along the top of a field to a metal farm gate with a blue waymarker; continue

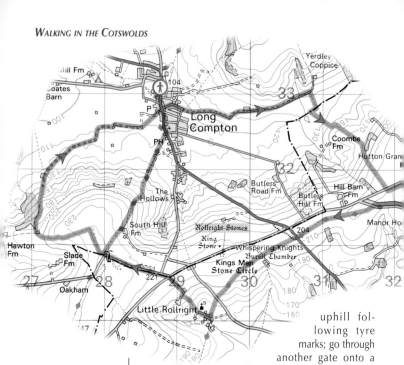

uphill fol-
lowing tyre
marks; go through
another gate onto a
farm track and take the next
left through a metal farm gate and into a walled field –
that doesn't have an obvious path, but you should find
a stile at the far side. (If in doubt just aim for the road.)

Cross the road, go into a field and take a left to
follow its edge. Enter the trees and turn right to head
towards **Great Rollright**, running parallel with the road.
Just before you reach another road, turn right, staying
inside the trees; again, parallel to a road.

It could be easy to miss the next turning. After about
ten minutes, when the path starts to go uphill, on almost
the crest of a hill, leave the woods to the left. Cross
the road to go through a metal kissing-gate by two old
wooden gates, signposted the d'Arcy Dalton Way, on a
broad path between hedges.

Go over a stile into a big field, with a big view opening up ahead, and stick to the hedge on the right. After

another field cross a road and go up steps and into the field on the right. Cross a track and carry on between trees, then out into a field and finally the good stuff: turn right to reach the **Whispering Knights Burial Chamber**.

This early Neolithic **burial chamber** – a portal dolman-style tomb – probably dates to around 4000–3000BC. There are similar examples in Cornwall, Wales and Ireland and it seems it was designed to impress. Bones were deposited here well into the Bronze Age and legend has it the stones were knights plotting against their king, so a witch turned them all into stone.

From here follow a clear path around the top of the field to the King's Men Stone Circle.

This ceremonial **stone circle** probably dates from the late Neolithic period. The pitted stones are irregularly spaced around a 30-metre diameter and some of the lichens are thought to be 400–800 years old. It's the easternmost stone circle in Britain and there are similar circles in the Lake District, Ireland and Wales. There are around 70 stones – it's

The Whispering Knights Burial Chamber. Did a witch do this?

thought originally there were 105 – and if you can count them three times in a row and get the same total you're the lucky recipient of... a wish.

Cross the road to find the King Stone.

The age of the large, lonely **King Stone** is unclear, as is its purpose, however it's probably from the middle Bronze Age. Like Stonehenge's Hele Stone it points towards the rising sun. The seal balancing a ball-style shape is due to 19th-century drovers who chipped off small pieces as lucky charms thought to keep the Devil at bay.

From here, unfortunately you need to retrace your steps all the way back to the stile before the Whispering Knights (sorry!). Once there, turn right to go across the middle of the field on an obvious path. Carry on in the same direction and the path starts to descend to **Little Rollright**. Cross a lane, then follow a path between hedges. At another lane turn right, signposted to the Manor House and Church, on a track, leaving the d'Arcy Dalton Way but briefly joining Shakespeare's Way. Go past the squat, 15th-century **church** and turn right, uphill, between young beach trees.

Bear right slightly to continue uphill to the left of some barns. At the road junction, cross over the first road and go up the road in front of you, which angles left. When the road corners left, leave it and go straight on through a metal gate. ◀

You can take a shorter route back to Long Compton, along the Macmillan Way, by turning right here.

The path swings to the right, sticking to the hedge. At the end of the field, turn left and downhill, again sticking to the hedge. At farm buildings, between gateposts, go right (not through the gate in front), leaving a bridleway and joining a public footpath. Go through a kissing-gate and downhill on a broad, grassy track. Aim at a couple of big barns and follow a bridlepath through fields for about 20 minutes back to **Long Compton**, emerging near the **church**.

WALK 5

Winchcombe, Hailes Abbey and Sudeley Castle

Start/Finish	Anywhere on B4632 (main road), Winchcombe (SP 026 285)
Distance	19km (12 miles)
Grade	3
Time	6hrs
Maps	OS Landranger 163 and 150 or Explorer OL45
Refreshments	Cafés and pubs in Winchcombe; Sudeley Castle (entry fee)
Public transport	Buses from Cheltenham (North Place)
Parking	Pay and display car parks in town or (for free) in nearby housing estates

This long circuit includes plenty of history and vistas. Leave infectious Winchcombe (for more info on the town, see Walk 6) to amble across undulating fields on the Cotswold/Winchcombe Way to the remains of 13th-century Hailes Abbey (entry fees apply). Then on to the Edge, on a pretty section of the Cotswold Way, with earthworks and gratifying views. A meandering route, along parts of the Warden's Way, brings you back to Winchcombe via Sudeley Castle (entry fees apply) and its extraordinary gardens.

Head north (towards Stratford) along the B4632 (also called High St, Hailes St and Broadway Rd). Just outside town look for a wooden Cotswold Way (CW) sign pointing you across the road and right, up Puck Pit Lane (also now the **Winchcombe Way**). Stay on the lane for some time as it ascends, getting greener and quieter. Carry on through a series of fields, uphill then flat, on a small but obvious path.

At a lane turn left. At a tarmac lane turn right, then left, onto a stony track (by The Barn). At a road turn right to visit **Hailes Abbey** (you can get a decent glimpse without paying).

The **Cistercian abbey of Hailes** was founded in 1246 by Earl Richard of Cornwall, brother of King Henry III, in thanks for surviving a shipwreck. It housed the Holy Blood of Hailes, claimed to be a phial of Christ's blood (however, later the king's commissioners alleged it was duck's blood) and it became a pilgrimage site. Since the Dissolution in 1539, when many religious institutions in England were closed or destroyed, only a few of the cloister arches and foundations remain, however, one Cistercian drain still works 750 years later. **www. nationaltrust. org.uk**

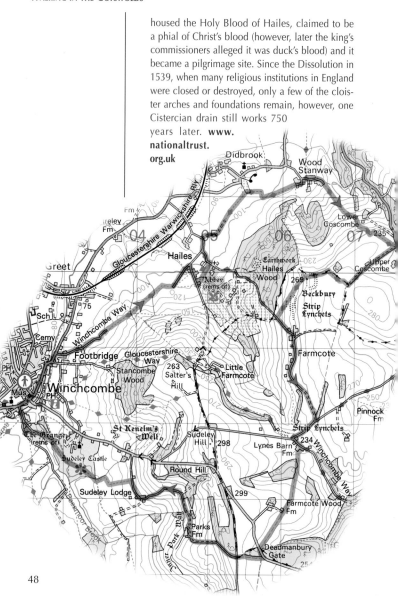

When you're done with the Abbey, retrace your steps and go past a little 12th-century Norman **church** (which has a number of medieval wall paintings and stained glass rescued from the Abbey) then turn right at the road junction. When the road bends left leave it to the right on a farm track signposted Winchcombe Way (WW). Go left on the track by an oak tree. At a kissing-gate go right. Go right by a rickety stile and stick to the right where the path seems to divide just inside the field. As the path peters out go across the middle of the field to reach a metal farm gate.

In the next field, follow contours round to the left, aiming for three water troughs and a gate. In the next, aiming at houses. Go through a gate to a lane by a house in **Wood Stanway** and follow the road round to the left. Then right at the junction by a WW sign and you're soon rejoining the Cotswold Way as you continue on that road.

The road goes uphill, then turns right by stables and the track continues uphill past farm buildings. Look for wooden waymarkers with acorn symbol to guide you through fields – head directly up the hill in the first big field, to the left of the lone oak tree, to a kissing-gate.

After the next gate, angle right to go uphill to another little gate, and another wooden gate, by a metal farm gate. Follow a wide grassy track, looking for waymarkers and uphill on a smaller track to a very inviting bench and some fantastic views.

Turn left to walk along the plateau edge following CW waymarkers. At the road by **Stumps Cross** turn immediately right. Follow a wide track (Campden Lane, a former sheep-drove road) and go right when it divides. Go through a metal farm gate into a field. Turn diagonally right and head for the bottom left-hand corner of the field, by some young trees. Go through a gate and follow the wall, past the earthworks of **Beckbury Camp** on the left, then on to the monument by beach trees.

There are remains of a four-acre **Iron Age promontory fort** at Beckbury Camp. A clear rampart and part-filled ditch can be seen – you can also see how the escarpment was used as a defensive aid. There are strip lynchets (ridges indicating a site of prehistoric ploughing) in the next field, too. Legend has it that by the nearby monument, Thomas Cromwell sat to watch the destruction of Hailes Abbey (although the monument was built later).

Go downhill and diagonally left across the field. Go through a wooden gate and slightly right to another gate by the corner of a copse. Go over a stile and continue in the same direction, now downhill. At a track leave the CW and turn left, uphill. The track leads through buildings and becomes a lane – continue on it for some time.

At a junction turn right, downhill, signposted Winchcombe. At the next junction turn left, where it says 'Unsuitable For Motors'. Leave the road to the right over a stile by a bridleway sign just after **Lynes Barn Farm** and follow a stony track right and uphill. At a junction near the top of hill continue in the same direction but onto a grassy track following a wall. The track shrinks to a footpath. Turn left at the road and you're soon joined by the Warden's Way, which takes you all the way back to Winchcombe.

You soon leave the road, onto a track on the right. Then a quick right, off the track and onto a footpath between a fence and trees. At a tarmac lane turn left then

Poppies in fields above Sudeley Castle

Sudeley Castle is the burial place of Catherine Parr, sixth wife of Henry VIII

quickly right onto a track. Before you reach trees turn right onto a stony track. Back on tarmac turn right along a pleasant country lane halfway up the valley-side.

Just before farm buildings turn right, onto a track. Turn right at the road but quickly left, downhill, into a field. Cross a stile, a ditch and turn right, along the right-hand edge of the next field, with **Sudeley Castle** ahead.

> The current **Sudeley Castle** – a manor house rather than bona fide castle – was built in the 15th century but on the site of a 12th-century castle. It's the burial place of Catherine Parr, sixth wife of Henry VIII, and is one of the few 'castles' left in England still a residence. The biggest reason for visiting is the gloriously colourful gardens, billowing with hundreds of varieties of roses and many other pretty things. There's plenty on the site's history, exhibitions, a coffee shop and an adventure playground. **www.sudeleycastle.co.uk**

Follow the field round to the left and across another stile. After a few metres of track, go over a stile on right. Turn half-left and go diagonally across a large field, passing the Castle, to a kissing-gate in the right-hand corner. Follow a wire fence on the right and go through two gates and onto a drive. Turn left towards **Winchcombe** (or right to visit the Castle). Turn right when the drive meets a road, which brings you back onto Winchcombe's B4632.

WALK 6

Winchcombe, Cleeve Common and Belas Knap

Start/Finish	Winchcombe church (B4632, main road through town) (SP 024 283)
Distance	12.5km (8 miles)
Grade	2
Time	3.5hrs
Maps	OS Landranger 163 or Explorer OL45 and 179
Refreshments	Pubs and cafés in Winchcombe
Public transport	Buses from Cheltenham (North Place)
Parking	Winchcombe has paid and free (if you look around) parking

Arguably the finest walk in the Cotswolds – and including, perhaps not coincidentally, the hill-chain's highest point and the biggest area of common land (so you may wander freely). Leave likeable Winchcombe for a stiff climb up Cleeve Common for vast views, before visiting the atmospheric Neolithic long barrow of Belas Knap. There's a sustained ascent and a long descent and the route follows parts of the Cotswold Way, the Winchcombe Way and the Gustav Holst Way, so signage is good.

Winchcombe was once the capital of the Anglo-Saxon kingdom of Mercia, but nowadays Winchcombe has the equally prestigious, if unofficial, title of the capital of walking in the Cotswolds. The Cotswold, Warden's, Windrush and Gloucestershire Ways all call into town, as does the 42-mile Winchcombe Way. The ancient Salt Way trading route went near here, hence a Salter's Lane and Salter's Hill, while Winchcombe Church has spectacular gargoyles and Civil War bulletmarks from where Royalist prisoners were shot dead. There are also village stocks outside the Folk Museum (hopefully no longer in use, but don't drop any litter just in case).

From the **church**, walk along B4632 (the main road) heading south-west out of town until you see a brown tourist sign for Belas Knap on the left. Take that little road and as it quickly bends right, leave it going straight on into a field through a kissing-gate by a sign for Cleeve Common. Then take a quick left through another kissing-gate to join a path between fences.

Leave the path, continuing in the same direction on a track, with a bizarrely coloured man-made pool on left. Pass carefully through a collection of workshops at **Postlip**. Follow green public footpath signs between and around buildings, going right and uphill, then left and back down, then up again through a small car park, turning right to leave the industrial unpleasantness behind.

Soon leave the track to the right by a waymarker, to go briefly into woods, but look almost immediately for a concrete slab-bridge on the left to go over a stream, then through a kissing-gate and into a field. Turn right and follow the bottom of the field uphill. Go over a stile, continuing in same direction on a muddy path between fences. Cross a road and go through a gate with a blue

4/7/16
* → WINCHCOMBE (HOLST WAY)

53

Cotswold Way (CW) marker. Follow the wall around and through a series of gates and between farm buildings, guided by blue CW pointers. The final gate, by the corner of a wall, spits you out onto **Cleeve Common**.

CLEEVE COMMON

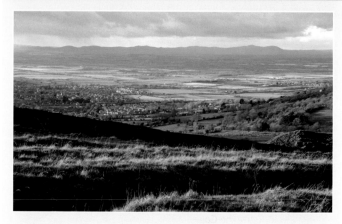

Views across the Vale of Evesham to the Malverns, from Cleeve Common

Our Neolithic friends first cleared the trees from Cleeve Common around 6000 years ago and there is evidence of prehistoric and Roman settlements. It's the largest area of unimproved limestone grassland in Gloucestershire and, along with Leckhampton Hill, has the thickest sections of exposed Jurassic rocks in the country, hence it's a Site of Special Scientific Interest. The remains of an Iron Age hillfort, dating from around 500BC (in the north-western corner of the Common, above the unsettlingly named settlement of Nutterswood), is three acres and a rough quarter-circle. There's a cross dyke too, a territorial boundary probably from the Bronze Age. You may find musk orchids (and four other species) and even glow-worms here, while roe and muntjac deer, stoats, weasels and hares all call the common home. Bird life includes meadow pipits, finches, linnet, yellowhammers, fieldfares, jackdaws, buzzards, kestrel – even ring ouzel, stonechat, wheatear and great grey shrike have been seen. It's also one of the few locations where the Duke of Burgundy butterfly can still be found in abundance.

Continue in the same direction, going through a metal gate. Continue on a track through another metal gate. By a building the CW goes left and uphill with big views opening up – of the Vale of Evesham and more. There's a spiders web of paths around here and as it's common land it's not too important which you take.

There's plenty to be said for following the CW along the western side of Cleeve Common. But while the views are bigger, they include Cheltenham and Gloucester, an eastern traverse along what's now the Winchcombe Way gives more intimate, greener views. To go this way, look for the prominent stony track, which goes left (soon branching away from the CW) and follow it for some time as it curves southeast. Although you'll probably want to detour right a little way for a rather outstanding trig point, from where, on a good day, you can see Shropshire, 72km away.

The track becomes covered with grass near the **telecommunications towers** but it's still reasonably easy to follow. ▶ Ignore other paths and head straight on, beginning to go downhill, passing a wooden post to reach a gate (with markers for the Winchcombe and Gustav Holst Ways) in the wall. Leave the Common on a stony path following a wall. The path levels out then goes downhill in the next field, towards abandoned farm buildings. Turn left after the barn and ignore a CW sign on the left. Turn right at the next CW sign, heading into a field and towards **Belas Knap**.

Southeast of the towers is the highest point in the Cotswolds (330m) but sadly it's an anticlimactic spot without views and barely worth a detour.

Belas Knap is a particularly fine example of a Neolithic long barrow and it's thought to be 5500 years old. At least 38 people were buried in the four chambers and they probably lived as cattle-herders, farmers and hunters. Animal bones and flints were also buried in the tomb, along with Roman coins and pottery. The entrance on the far right was a false one (in contrast Uley and Nympsfield long barrows have strongly emphasised entrances with chambers opening out on either side of a central passage), used for ceremonies. Its inner walls were made in

Belas Knap

the same style of Cotswold drystone walls as is still used today. The name means 'hill-top beacon' and suggests the Saxons used the site.

To exit, go over a stile opposite where you came in, then turn immediately left to follow a path by a wall. The path descends and goes through a metal kissing-gate. Continue next to the wall, turning left at the bottom of the field to reach the far corner. Go through a kissing-gate and downhill into trees. Go left at the bottom, staying in the trees.

Go through a gate and cross the road, up the bank to a gate, then straight down the middle of a big field, towards Winchcombe. Go through a kissing-gate to join a lane, turning right onto it. At a bigger lane turn left. At a signpost on the right, go through kissing-gate and into field, following the CW through fields back into **Winchcombe** via Vineyard Street (which used to be Duck Street, named after a ducking stool in the River Isborne).

WALK 7

Temple Guiting, Guiting Wood and Guiting Power

Start/Finish	Post office and shop, Temple Guiting (SP 094 282)
Distance	11.5km (7 miles)
Grade	1
Time	3hrs
Maps	OS Landranger 163 or Explorer OL45
Refreshments	Farmers Arms, Ye Olde Inne, Guiting Power; Half Way House, Kineton
Public transport	Very limited bus service from Stow-on-the-Wold and Cheltenham
Parking	Limited parking opposite the post office and shop

A deliciously quiet stroll – the Cotswolds don't feel like a tourist honeypot here. Starting from shy Temple Guiting descend into a pretty wooded valley, up through ever-changing, wildlife-populated Guiting Wood, then into another coy valley and cute Power Guiting. It's across leisurely fields and a quiet lane through Kineton and back to the start. There are only minor hill-climbs and although there's a fair bit of lane walking, they're quiet and often tree-clad. This route has probably the easiest navigation in the book and includes parts of the Winchcombe Way, Warden's Way, Gustav Holst Way and Diamond Way. You could push on along the Winchcombe Way, north, to handsome little Ford and loop back round via the ancient site of Dinnock Village.

From the post office and shop, come back out to the main road and turn left. You're soon joined by the Winchcombe Way as you go downhill and across the River Windrush. As you start to ascend, look for the **church** on your left and take a path to its right between a wall and hedge.

> **Guiting** comes from the Saxon word 'gye-ting', which refers somehow to the nearby River Windrush. The Knights Templar religious organisation used to own the village, hence the name, and the church dates from the 12th-century. There's the

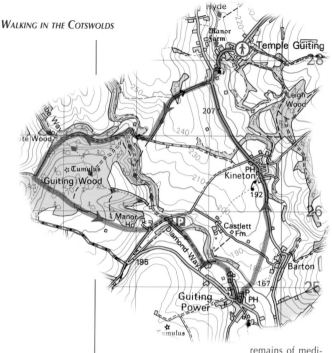

remains of medieval glass in the middle window on the south side; New York's Metropolitan Museum of Art has nabbed some of it.

At the lane, cross over and go uphill on a lane signposted 'Unsuitable for Motors'. At the crest of the hill look out for the giant grasshopper and continue on, downhill into a peaceful multi-fold valley, where you may see birds of prey.

At a junction turn right and go downhill towards the wooded valley-bottom. Cross a stream on a pretty, hazel-arched lane and follow it uphill. When the road swings right, go through the grey kissing-gate of the Farmcote Estate, and turn right, now on the Warden's Way, to follow the brown fence on a track.

Keep on till you meet a wood on the right and a crossroads, with a cabal of yellow waymarkers on a

fence. Turn left here, going uphill into the trees, on a smaller path. Stick to the path over a couple of crossroads as the woods thin out to reach a Farmcote Estate kissing-gate. Leaving the wood, turn left and follow the edge of the wood through a couple of fields.

A concertina of hill folds and valleys, near Temple Guiting

At a corner at the end of the second field continue in the same direction going steeply downhill into the valley. At the drive to the **Manor House** turn right and follow to the lane. Turn left to go into Kineton Public Road. ▶

Where a track crosses the lane, just before a small stone building, turn right and go downhill on the Gustav Holst Way (also the Warden's Way and **Diamond Way**). At a T-junction where you meet a lane go left and down-hill, passing a couple of barns. Stick to the right-hand side of the river as the track climbs again and goes through a natural tree-arch. The path becomes a lane as you enter unreasonably handsome **Guiting Power**.

Excavations around here uncovered the remnants of an Iron Age farm dating from around the third to first centuries BC.

Half of **Guiting Power**'s un-Cotswoldy name comes from a pre-eminent local family, Le Poers, back in the day. The village is in the Domesday Book and indeed you feel you've stepped back in time here. Guiting Power did well from the wool trade and it's still a handsome place – friendly, too. Commendably, the Guiting Manor Amenity Trust owns and manages much of the village, renting houses to local people, meaning they can afford to keep living here, unusual in the Cotswolds, where local people are often priced out. The village green was the site of regular markets and St Michael's Church has Norman origins. Descendants of the Cotswold Lion can be seen at the Cotswold Farm Park. **www.cotswoldfarmpark.co.uk**

Turn left at a T-junction to reach the village centre, by a Post Office and war memorial. Turn left just before the phone box imprisoned in the wall, going downhill. Go through a wooden kissing-gate and cross a track to take the smaller path in front going downhill next to a stream. Go over a footbridge and uphill slightly. Take the left option of two kissing-gates and into a field with a hedge on your right.

At a lane, with little **Barton** on your right, cross over, and continue on through two fields. Go over a stile and onto a lane and turn left. Simply follow this quiet lane through **Kineton** and, before you know it, back to **Temple Guiting**.

A natural tree arch, just before entering Guiting Power

WALK 8

Bourton-on-the-Water,
the Slaughters and Naunton

Start/Finish	Large pay and display car park, Bourton-on-the-Water (SP 170 208)
Distance	16km (10 miles)
Grade	2
Time	5hrs
Maps	OS Landranger 163 or Explorer OL45
Refreshments	Cafés and pubs in Bourton-on-the-Water; The Slaughters Inn and Old Mill, both Lower Slaughter; Black Horse, Naunton
Public transport	Buses from Cheltenham (Beachwood Centre)

If you're pining for the classic/clichéd syrupy Cotswold village experience, this is for you. After the 'Venice of the Cotswolds' come the Slaughters, which in the seminal 1933 travelogue *English Journey* JB Priestley said, 'They should be preserved forever the way they are now', and they feel like they have been (he wasn't so enthused about Bourton). Plus there are some bashful, shallow valleys to enjoy. The first part follows the well-signposted Warden's Way, then parts of the Gustav Holst Way. If you've visited Bourton-on-the-Water (avoid summer and weekends, and especially summer weekends) previously or prefer crowd-dodging, you could cut it out altogether, starting out from one of the other villages. A walk best suited to the offseason.

The '**Venice of the Cotswolds**' is certainly hand-some but probably the most visited place in the region. Its pretty, inviting greens, backed by Jacobean and Georgian stonemasonry and split by the tree-lined River Windrush and its five pho-togenic little footbridges (built in the mid-1800s) make the High Street a sweetly perfect sight. You won't struggle for ice creams, cream teas or post-cards around here.

Turn right, out of the car park, and take the next right, onto High Street, the main tourist area. When you see a

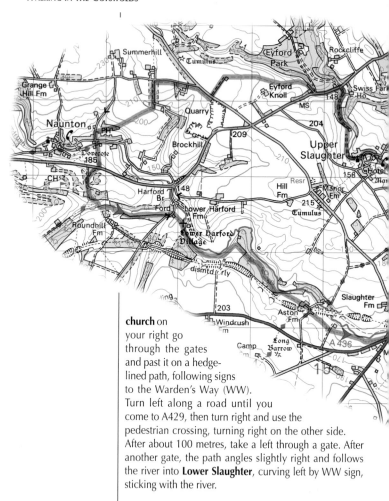

church on your right go through the gates and past it on a hedge-lined path, following signs to the Warden's Way (WW). Turn left along a road until you come to A429, then turn right and use the pedestrian crossing, turning right on the other side. After about 100 metres, take a left through a gate. After another gate, the path angles slightly right and follows the river into **Lower Slaughter**, curving left by WW sign, sticking with the river.

The word **slaughter** means 'marshy place' rather than anything more sinister. That said, Lower Slaughter, smaller and better-looking than Bourton, with its punctilious honeycomb riverside cottages, has an unmistakable *Midsomer Murders* vibe. Copse Hill Road was voted Most Romantic Street in Britain on a Google Street View poll (for what that's worth). Neighbouring Upper Slaughter, tucked pleasingly into the landscape and with its Saxon church, isn't as immediately picturesque but is perhaps more pleasing for it.

At the road by a bridge, cross over, keeping the river to your left, as the path swings round to the old mill, now a museum (and seller of organic ice cream). Go left after the mill between buildings and hedges. Follow a clear footpath with the river on the left, then through fields. In the third field go downhill to a small stone footbridge and follow a path left between a fence and hedge into **Upper Slaughter**.

Go left at the road and right at a road junction. After a red phone box turn left by a bench (into 'No Through Road'). Go through a gate as the path goes uphill, then descends. Pass a cottage on your right and continue on the obvious track into woods. Continue in same direction when track meets lane.

At the road, turn left and cross with care. After 300 metres turn right, past cottages on a stony track (not uphill on tarmac) by a WW signpost. In the field stick to the wall on the left to go uphill. Go through gates, heading for farm buildings. Follow signs through the farmyard and turn left onto a track which leads to a road.

The Old Mill, Lower Slaughter

Cross the road, go through a gate and turn right. Stick to the right-hand-side of a field, following wall and road, as the path goes over a stile, crosses a track (to Brockhill Farm), through three gates and past a farm so new it's not on some maps. One more gate, then turn left onto a track and downhill on the WW.

When the track bends left, continue in the same direction on a path, downhill into trees. The path ascends into fields on a clear path with great views. After a blue waymarker, go into trees and through a gate, downhill towards **Naunton**, another pretty village, and quieter still than the Slaughters.

At the lane turn left. At a T-junction (the **Black Horse pub** is just metres to your left) go almost straight across, up a drive between houses and over a footbridge, then uphill between, to reach a road. Turn right at the road and after about 80 metres cross over and follow green bridleway and Gustav Holst Way (GHW) signs on track, with golf course on the right. Go downhill and steeply into a pretty valley. Cross a stream and head left, follow the stream along the valley bottom for ten minutes or so.

When a gate leads to a lane go straight over (now on the Windrush Way as well as GHW). Go over a small hill, then a stile and continue to follow the valley bottom. Go over two stiles and through a gate as the valley bends left. At a fork take the right, going uphill between gorse bushes. Go through a gate and across a field, keeping to the trees on the left, then downhill and into woods.

Follow a clear path for some time. After emerging in a field, go through **Aston Farm** and ignore the first left (along the Windrush Way). Take the second left up a broad track between hedges. Go through a big field, cross a farm track and go over the stile opposite, looking for a narrow path down the middle of a field. Go through trees and a kissing-gate, then follow the field to a gate through the conifers. Turn left and cross the busy **A429** with care. Just after the bridge, turn right into Lansdowne Road. Follow the road to High Street.

The path into Naunton (and a welcome, half-way pub)

WALK 9
Leckhampton Hill and Crickley Hill

Start/Finish	Lay-by on A436 near the junction with A435 near Seven Springs (SO 967 169)
Distance	16.5km (10 miles)
Grade	3
Time	5hrs
Maps	OS Landranger 163 or Explorer 179
Refreshments	Snack van in lay-by; Star Bistro café, near Ullenwood; Air Balloon pub, Crickley Hill (public toilets at Crickley Hill)
Public transport	Buses from Cheltenham (Promenade) to Birdlip (then start from Air Balloon pub)
Parking	The layby at the start/finish of the walk

One of the very best parts of the Cotswold Way, this route includes two prominent scarp spurs and four epic viewpoints. There's fascinating archaeology on Crickley Hill, while neighbouring Leckhampton has historical quarrying and the Devil's Chimney landmark. Lots of this route follows the Cotswold Way, which aids navigation, plus parts of the Gloucestershire Way. There's an unusual amount of road walking, ironically that's on the Cotswold Way. There's a delightful little valley near the end too.

Turn left out of the lay-by (where there's often a snack van). Stay left at the roundabouts until you meet a side-road, where you join the **Cotswold Way** (CW) – which you'll be following for some time. As the road swings left, go straight on down an obvious track in a tree tunnel. Go through a gate on the left and up Hartley Hill following a wall, as superlative views of the north Cotswolds open up ahead, with Cleve Common dominating, with Cheltenham below. Follow the Edge around the corner and you can see the Malverns ahead, and pass some inviting benches.

The path ducks and weaves among earthworks, but look for CW waymarkers or just stick loosely to the Edge, as you pass a trig point and reach a topograph, with more stunning views, across the Severn Vale to the Black Mountains.

LECKHAMPTON HILL

Leckhampton Hill trig point and big views across the Vale of Gloucester to Wales

Along with Cleeve Common, Leckhampton Hill has the thickest sections of exposed Jurassic rocks in the country. An Iron Age hillfort and barrow tell us this hill has long been used by Cotswolds folk. Sheep were farmed here in medieval times, while the Jurassic limestone was quarried by the Romans. Just below the Edge, the Devil's Chimney is the result of extensive 18th-century quarrying. Climbing used to be allowed on the pointy crag but not now as repair work has been needed to avert collapse. You can also see ruins of lime kilns. Naturalist Dr Edward Wilson, who died by Captain Robert Scott's side in Antarctica, was raised in Cheltenham and spent much of his youth at Crippetts Farm, Leckhampton. In summer you may see tree pipits, yellow-hammers, willow warblers and buzzards up here, while winter brings red wings and fieldfares. Roe deer, foxes, badgers, lizards, adders, plus moths, 33 species of butterfly and (including small blue and common blue) even glow-worms live in this Local Nature Reserve too.

Continue following the Edge and the CW. ▶ When the path divides stay on the higher route, reaching a road. Turn left and uphill. Turn right when the wall ends, onto a track for around 15 minutes. At the next road go right, passing Star Bistro café. Cross a road with care and continue in the same direction. Follow the road till it starts to

There's a signed diversion down to the Devil's Chimney and the old quarries are worthy of exploration.

go downhill. Take a left by a CW signpost up steps and into beech woods.

Go through gates (trying to spot the conifer-topped mound of Crippets Neolithic **long barrow** on the left) and onto **Crickley Hill** proper, staying on the right of a fence. At a split in the path take the higher route, up steps and into woods again, with glimpses of spectacular views. After a wooden gate turn right to follow a wall uphill. Take a right through a gate and out towards the Edge. Stick to the higher path where route gets vague and follow waymarkers through car park and past toilets.

People first lived at the super-scenic spot of **Crickley Hill** in 4000BC, although there have been at least three separate settlements here (Iron Age, Romans, Dark Ages and maybe Bronze Age too). The information boards do a good job of explaining more about the inhabitants' lives, which judging by the amount of arrowheads and charred remains found, dated to 3450BC, weren't entirely peaceful. Over half the National Trust-owned hill is a Site of Special Scientific Interest. Orchids, rare fungi (don't touch) and deadly nightshade (ditto – extremely poisonous) are also found up here. Gloucester-born poet and musician Ivor Gurney wrote a poignant poem entitled *Crickley Hill* when he was stationed in France in World War I, including the lines:

O sudden steep! Oh hill towering above!
Chasm from the road falling suddenly away!
Sure no men talked of you with more love.

From a topograph you can see Cooper's Hill (Walk 11), May Hill, the Black Mountains and even Shropshire's Brown Clee Hill, 72km away. Go through a gate by the wall and start downhill, past obvious earthworks on the left and pretty views to right – of where you're heading. CW waymarkers guide you through the mature woodland with some imperious beech, and gradually downhill to the road.

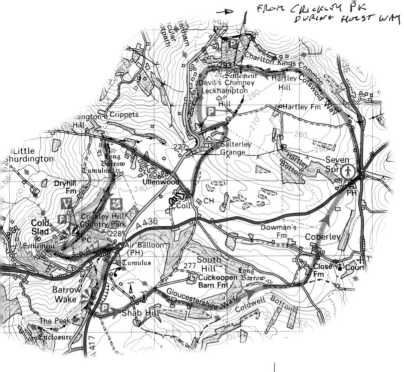

(handwritten annotation at top: FROM CRICKLEY PK DURING HORST WAY)

Cross the busy road towards the Air Balloon pub, and uphill on the pavement to the left of it. After a telephone box, turn right, then right into woods, then out again along **Barrow Wake**. ▸ Enjoy more big views, including back to Crickley Hill. Continue along the Edge but keep an eye out for the end of the car park above, where you need to cross the road and go under the bridge. Follow the lane. Continue across another lane and between **communications towers** and turn right at Rushwood Kennels and Cattery, down their drive, now on the **Gloucestershire Way**. Keep the barking cages on your left to locate a yellow marker and track between two fences. The track becomes a narrow path, then a wider path between trees in a pretty valley. Just before a metal gate and stile turn left onto a clear path.

Various treasures were found in a female burial site here: bronze owls, a decorative bucket and the remarkable Birdlip Mirror, now in Gloucester City Museum – the original site is now under the road.

69

Walking along Barrow Wake with Crickley Hill behind

After a gate, by the mounds of a **long barrow**, turn right to join a track going downhill. Continue in the same direction when the track meets a lane. Ignore the first left, take the next one, through a gate and onto a track. Ignore a path to the right and go through kissing-gates down to a footbridge, then uphill to a road in **Coberley**.

Turn right then left to go past a telephone box and slightly uphill. Angle right to go past a school and leave the tarmac by a sign for Leckhampton Hill on a clear path by a hedge taking you into fields. Continue through several fields in the same direction until you reach the busy **A436**. Turn right, then cross with care to find the lay-by.

WALK 10

*Chedworth, Withington
and the Roman Villa*

Start/Finish	St Andrew's Church, northern end of Chedworth (SO 052 121)
Distance	13km (8 miles)
Grade	2
Time	4hrs
Maps	OS Landranger 163 or Explorer OL45
Refreshments	Seven Tuns pub, Chedworth; Mill Inn, Withington; café at Chedworth Roman Villa
Public transport	Buses from Cirencester (London Road)
Parking	Available by the church

A walk for wood fans, admirers of enchanting valleys – the Coln Valley is one of the most enchanting in the Cotswolds – and anyone interested in seeing one of the finest Roman mosaics in the country (entry fees apply; closed in winter; www.nationaltrust.org.uk). There's little gradient and the walk includes parts of the Macmillan Way.

Go through the churchyard, uphill to the left of the **church** (which has Norman origins), and over a stile into a field. Go over a stone stile at the top-right corner of the field. After an avenue of beech trees, take a right by a Manor Farm sign to go along a track. Go over a stile and continue in the same direction.

Just after two metal gates, the track swings left. Look for stile in front that takes you angling right through a field and across an atmospheric old airfield. Cross stiles until you're on an old runway. When you reach the corner of a fence on the left, swing left to roughly follow the fence and runway, angling gradually right/across it, to reach a fence by the road and go through a kissing-gate.

Cross the road, go over a stile onto a track and turn right by a metal gate, down a narrow path between a fence and hedge. Just inside a little wood go left. Go into a field, over a stile, cross a road and go down a track to

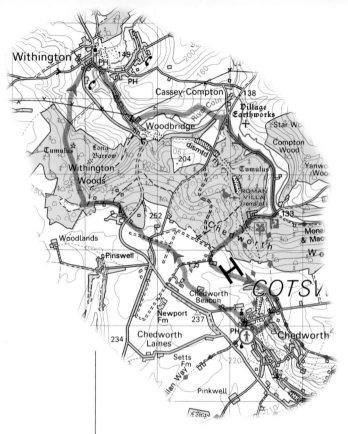

the right of a **communications tower**, along the edge of woods, passing a cottage on the left.

Ignore tracks on the right until, in a clearing, take a well-signposted right, downhill on a broad track into the woods proper. The map shows a **long barrow**, **tumulus** and cross dyke in these woods, while hazel trees have been coppiced and woodland is constantly changing. ◄

By an old metal gate stay on the same path (ignoring a right turn). The path levels out and just after two right turns, turn right at a T-junction. The path goes steeply downhill to a metal gate, out of the wood and into a pretty valley. Follow yellow waymarkers left,

There is sometimes shooting here so keep to paths.

then diagonally down the field to go through the wall under electricity cables. Carry on in the same direction to a wooden gate in the dip. Continue to the bottom left-hand corner of field and the road. Turn left into **Withington**.

Turn right at the first road junction. At the next, turn left to go past the inviting pub garden of the **Mill Inn**. Follow the road round to the left and leave it by a sign-post going up steps on the right after a telephone box.

Follow the narrow path into a thicket. Go over a stile to enter the garden of Riverside Cottage (but be wary of crocodiles). Turn left up the drive, then right along a lane. Turn left under a railway bridge and uphill to the right, then left over a stile and into a field. Follow a hedge then go over a stile into a thicket.

Leave the lovely corridor of trees and continue next to hawthorns, going gradually uphill. This is the prettiest part of the walk (if you ignore the electrical pylons), in the beautiful, discreet Coln Valley. At a track by a wooden gate turn right and downhill. Go over a stile at the bottom of the field and cross the **River Coln**, then go left on a track in a field, and uphill. Ignore two sets of tracks that

Light at the end of the Withington Woods tunnel

cross the path as it swings right and continues uphill, but then seems to disappear. Continue to follow what feels like an ancient ditch to the top right corner of the field and a stile. At the road, turn left and downhill, turning right at a junction. Follow the road for some time, with the River Coln on the left and **Chedworth Woods** on your right. At a road junction, turn right towards the **Roman Villa**.

> **Chedworth Roman Villa**, owned by the National Trust, dates from the second century AD although its heyday as one of the largest Romano-British villas in the country was the fourth century. The overgrown site was rediscovered in 1864 by a Victorian gamekeeper. Walkways allow close inspection of mosaics and there's insight into Roman bathhouses, latrines and underfloor heating. There's a café too. **www.nationaltrust.org.uk**

The path goes to the left of buildings and uphill. Go under a railway bridge and then steeply uphill. At a crossroads with a signpost in the middle, turn left, following the **Macmillan Way**. The path goes uphill and leaves the

Even on a grey day, Coln Valley is enchanting

woods through a gate, continuing straight on. At the top of the hill, by two gates, go left for the scenic route into charming Chedworth.

A view of Cassey Compton

Where several tracks meet, take the one in almost the same direction, between two fences. At the road, turn right and downhill. As the road swings right, turn left through a gate and downhill. Go through a gate with a 'Please close the gate' sign and angle right to go downhill, aiming for a kissing-gate by a cottage with a red chimney.

Cross the lane and continue downhill. Go over a stone stile and uphill. Go over another stile and briefly into trees. Go over another stile and turn right to go over yet another one straight away, sticking to the top/left of the field. Go over a stile by a gate that brings you round the back of the **Seven Tuns pub** (circa 1610). Turn right at the road and take footpath opposite pub to return to the church.

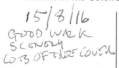

15/8/16
GOOD WALK
SCONERY
LOTS OF TREE COVER

WALK 11

*Cranham, Cooper's Hill
and Painswick Beacon*

Start/Finish	Car park, Cranham (SO 894 125)
Distance	11km (7 miles); shorter version 8km (5 miles)
Grade	2
Time	4hrs; shorter version 3hrs
Maps	OS Landranger 162 and 163 or Explorer 179
Refreshments	Black Horse Inn, Cranham
Public transport	Buses from Gloucester (bus station)

This walk's nature reserves include some of the finest examples of beech woodlands in Europe – it can feel like tunnels of fire in autumn. And when you finally emerge from trees, it's usually to see cracking views. You'll also visit the very steep Cooper's Hill, site of the world famous cheese rolling, with Painswick Beacon and the finest hillfort in the Cotswolds, plus an optional detour to the Great Witcombe Roman Villa. The route follows parts of the Cotswold Way and the Wysis Way, meaning navigation is good. Look for fallow dear in the woods and bluebells in spring.

Turn right out of the car park, then right again, to walk past the school. Go left on the **common** by the signpost for Scout HQ and Village Hall. By a telephone box, cross the road and onto a track.

When the track splits, go left, uphill into trees. Cross a footbridge and head uphill past a sign for **Buckholt Woods** and Rough Park Woods National Nature Reserve, which help conserve orchids, buzzards and silver-washed fritillary butterflies.

Ignore a track on the right as you see a clearing and carry on uphill on the stony path, which broadens out. Pass a house and turn left at the road. Take a quick right, onto a track that goes back into the trees and downhill.

Duck left off the track by private property on a stony path and past a nature reserve sign. Ignore a path to the right just after and you'll soon meet the **Cotswold Way** (CW), which you'll be on for some time. Turn left. At a

VAGUE

(handwritten note) DIRECTIONS CULD BE BETTER AT TIMES

fork, take the lower path to the right. ▶ Otherwise, take the left, uphill. The track passes a house, as you start to get views along the escarpment, then spits you out onto tarmac by houses. Follow the road as it swings to the left and, by a red post box, look for a left turning left to take you underneath famous **Cooper's Hill**.

Cooper's Hill was part of a sizeable Iron Age encampment. Nowadays, with its dilapidated sign and rickety wooden fences, you'd hardly know it was a world famous bit of hillside. On Spring Bank Holiday, a mock double Gloucester cheese is rolled down the precipitous slope and people run/fall after it, usually gaining new injuries while someone from nearby Brockworth nabs the prize. TV crew are sent from the world over to cover it and up to 15,000 people attend. The idiosyncratically Cotswoldian

A sign offers a detour to the Great Witcombe Roman Villa (the remains of a large villa built around AD250), a quarter of a mile away.

The vertiginous view from the top of Cooper's Hill of cheese rolling fame. Yes. Down that

event has been celebrated for centuries and is thought to have its roots in a heathen festival. **www. cheese-rolling.co.uk**

Go through a wooden kissing-gate and past a sign for the Cooper's Hill Local Nature Reserve. In the woods go steeply uphill. At a fork follow the CW to the left and uphill. Angle left and uphill again by another waymarker. The last bit of ascent is a real calf-burner, but then you're atop Cooper's Hill, which looks much steeper from up here, but bequeaths triumphant views across the Severn Vale to the Malverns and Black Mountains. The perfect picnic spot (unless it's cheese rolling day).

Follow CW signs back into the trees and through a confusing meeting of paths. Go right at the next fork, still in the trees but between two fields. After a wooden kissing-gate go straight on. By the next waymarker take a sharp left.

When paths meet carry straight on, looking for a waymarker a little way ahead, and the path goes steeply uphill. Stick to the right at the top. The path flattens out and goes past a nature reserve sign in a lovely stretch of woodland. Go right at the junction just after the sign. At a road turn right. ▶

At the busy main road, cross with care and go straight into the woods by a waymarker. Briefly follow an old drystone wall, until a waymarker takes you left. Cross a road and back into our old friend the Buckholt Woods nature reserve, taking the path on the left. Leave the reserve and go onto a lane in the same direction. Go past a small car park on the right and turn off the lane onto a track in the same direction. Then turn off the track, left onto a path, by a wooden waymarker, which soon deposits you on **Painswick Beacon**. There's a golf course here; keep straight on and you'll start to see impressive mounds and shapes: the remains of the Cotswolds' best-looking **hillfort**. The path continues to the left of the fort, but it is well worth clambering up and exploring it – just look out for flying golf balls.

For the shorter version, follow the signpost left, along roads, for a mile's walk back to Cranham.

Striding atop Painswick Beacon's Iron Age hillfort

79

Painswick Beacon is home to the evocative remains of **Kimsbury Camp**, an Iron Age hillfort dating from around 400BC to AD43. Two, maybe three, lines of ramparts and ditches can still be clearly seen, while the interior was living quarters. The vantage point was also used as a camp in 1052 by Earl Godwyn, a Saxon leader fighting the Earl of Mercia, and again in 1643 by retreating Royalist forces after the Siege of Gloucester. Due to unfarmed limestone grasslands, despite the Romans possibly having quarried stone here to build Gloucester, and a golf course having been idiotically built on it, this is a Scheduled Ancient Monument and a Site of Special Scientific Interest. Look out for wild flowers, including musk orchids, and butterflies, such as marbled white, chalkhill blue, brown angus and grizzled skipper.

A rustly stretch of beech woodland

At the road turn left. At a junction of road and track, leave the CW and join the **Wysis Way**, which takes you into the trees. Cross a road and turn left and follow the

pavement to steps on the right. Follow a signpost across the lane and into fields. After a stile, a path weaves to the right and gradually downhill, then round to the left as the gradient steepens.

Cross a stream and a field, aiming to the left of the telegraph pole. Just inside trees cross a stile to the right and another stile takes you into a field. Cross a stile by the farm, and another, to go straight on between barns to cross a stream and another stile with a yellow marker. Angle left, with a stream on your left, and aim for the wooden stile just uphill from a gate, with **Saltridge Hill** towering in front of you.

After the wooden stile, leave the Wysis Way and turn left on the track, then immediately off it to the right, aiming for a stile at the end of the farm-property wall. Go through a wooden kissing-gate and turn right and downhill on a track. Go past a gorgeous weeping willow and house on the left, over a stile and into a field. Stick to the lower side of the field, aiming for the right of Tocknells Court. Go over a stile then footbridge and follow the edge of the field and stream (on your left) to a stile and a lane.

Carry on in the same direction, leaving the tarmac to the right just round the corner. Go over a small footbridge and through trees. Cross another footbridge, then a stile, to leave the trees. Go uphill, initially, and over the middle of the field towards a little house. Just before it, look in the hedge to the right for a partially hidden footbridge. Cross it, then go uphill in a field, through a gate and continue in same direction.

Go to the right of Mann's Court to find a stile on the left and onto the road. Turn left at the tarmac, then right on the road (ignore public footpath sign), signposted into **Cranham**. You'll soon reach the **church**.

WALK 12

Brimpsfield and Caudle Green

Start/Finish	Brimpsfield village hall (SO 937 127)
Distance	9km (5.5 miles)
Grade	2
Time	3.5hrs
Maps	OS Landranger 163 or Explorer 179
Refreshments	None
Public transport	Buses from Cheltenham
Parking	Free at village hall

Starting from pretty little Brimpsfield (with a 15th-century church), this is a peaceful ramble through secluded valleys and woods. Around half of it is in trees, there's very little gradient and it's similar terrain to Walks 14 and 17 – if slightly less memorable. A good option for when more popular places are bustling.

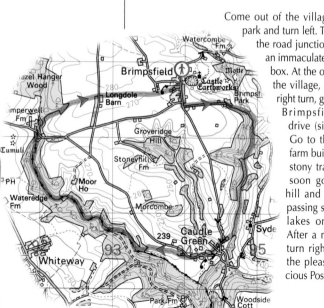

Come out of the village hall car park and turn left. Turn right at the road junction and pass an immaculate red phone box. At the other end of the village, just after a right turn, go left down Brimpsfield Park drive (signposted). Go to the right of farm buildings on a stony track, which soon goes downhill and into trees, passing some pretty lakes on the left. After a metal gate, turn right and into the pleasingly spacious Poston Wood.

Follow the whistling little stream on your right and just after crossing it turn left at a fork and through a wooden gate into a clearing. Follow the curve of the valley round (listen out for woodpeckers hammering away) to a metal gate. Cross a stream, go over a stile by a metal gate and follow the stream along the pretty valley bottom as the trees thin out. ▶ Go through a gate between two enormous evergreens, over a stile and past a cottage. Continue up the drive to a lane and turn left (ignoring a footpath on the right).

When the road swings left, take the stile over the wall to go steeply up a grass bank. Turn right at the lane into **Caudle Green** proper, continuing uphill through the comely village.

Look for a gateway on the left with a blue way-marker, then follow the wall on the right tracing the edge of a long field. When you reach the corner, turn left to follow the field edge down towards the wood. Take a right before the next wall, following a blue arrow on a wooden waymarker, into the trees and downhill.

Emerge briefly from the trees and stick to the left to go back into them on a track going downhill. At the

Walks don't get much quieter than Brimpsfield

To detour to the village of Syde, with its 12th-century church and 14th-century tithe barn, look for a path up to the left along here.

bottom take the track to the right of the pond. Ignore side-paths and stick to the main track, which follows a stream along the valley bottom. At a fork where the track goes left and over a stream, continue on by the blue bridleway marker in the same direction.

Go through a wooden gate, and the path goes uphill slightly by a clearing on the right. Go over a stile and back into the trees by some painted blue arrows and follow the track round to the right, rejoining the valley bottom.

At the road, cross over and go to the left of Climperwell Cottage into a field. Follow the wall around to the right. Before you reach a wall in front, swing right and uphill slightly to a wooden stile and back into the trees – albeit briefly.

Exit the trees and go through two fields to a lane. Cross over and take a track opposite between hedges. The track becomes a wide grassy path. After a beech-tree plantation, cross another track and go through a small wooden gate into a field to see **Brimpsfield** ahead of you.

Brimpsfield: it's a pig's life

WALK 13

Painswick, Edge and Painswick Beacon

Start/Finish	Reasonably priced pay and display car park, off A46, Painswick (SO 865 095)
Distance	12km (7.5 miles)
Grade	2
Time	4hrs
Maps	OS Landranger 162 or Explorer 179
Refreshments	Cafés and pubs in Painswick
Public transport	Buses from Stroud and Gloucester

Enjoy two charming, quiet valleys – including possibly the friendliest in the Cotswolds – before an assault on spectacular Painswick Beacon. The summit offers full 360-degree views and dramatic remains of Iron Age fortifications, arguably the finest in the region. The route incorporates lanes, field walking and quite a few hills, mostly short and sharp. It follows parts of the Cotswold Way, so signage is mostly good.

Go downhill and out of the car park, turning left onto Stamages Lane, and continuing downhill on a pretty, steep country lane. After a crossroads, at the bottom of the valley, turn right onto a signposted path by a river. Continue through a field, still following the river.

Go over a stile, footbridge, through a gate and turn left down a track between fences, by Kings Mill. The track goes uphill and when it meets a lane angle right. Continue through Gyde's Farm on a track between buildings and into a field. Head almost straight across, angling left a tad between hawthorn trees and a fence corner, to go downhill and across a footbridge. Go uphill, aiming for the right-hand corner of the field. In the next field go straight across, aiming at buildings. At a pretty lane turn right and go down a tunnel of hazel and beech.

At the road (**A46**), cross with great care (use the mirror) and go up Wragg Castle Lane. Turn right by a sign for Castle Farm, taking a track between houses – don't be put off by the lack of public footpath signs – and into a field.

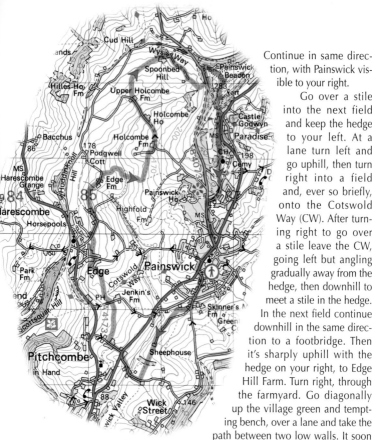

Continue in same direction, with Painswick visible to your right.

Go over a stile into the next field and keep the hedge to your left. At a lane turn left and go uphill, then turn right into a field and, ever so briefly, onto the Cotswold Way (CW). After turning right to go over a stile leave the CW, going left but angling gradually away from the hedge, then downhill to meet a stile in the hedge. In the next field continue downhill in the same direction to a footbridge. Then it's sharply uphill with the hedge on your right, to Edge Hill Farm. Turn right, through the farmyard. Go diagonally up the village green and tempting bench, over a lane and take the path between two low walls. It soon plonks you into fields with pretty views to the right. Continue in roughly the same direction to a lane and turn right.

Stick to the left at a road junction. At Edge Farm Cottage, ignore paths to right and left and go straight through the property. Continue through a field, over a stile and down towards **Edge Farm**, then left through it. Just outside the farm you're faced with possibly the biggest collection of gates you've ever seen. But don't be bamboozled. Just before them is a stile on the right – part-hidden by thorn bushes and the marker is nowhere to be seen too.

Painswick's famous church is on the horizon for much of this walk

Go over it, and another just after, into a steep field. Keep to the right to find a stile near the valley bottom.

After it, go left to find a footbridge and a narrow track between hedges. Go over a stile on the left into a field and roughly follow the contour to the right of the farm. In the next field stick to the hedge on the right to find a stile to a track. Turn right. The track becomes a lane and swings left (ignore a right turn). Go downhill and past pretty 16th-century **Holcombe House**. As the road bends left go right and over a stile into a field. Go up the middle, over some lumpy bits, with Painswick Beacon visible on the right, and head towards newly planted trees in the field's corner. Continue on the obvious broad path.

Go directly through Spoonbed Farm and uphill on a track, then right onto another track at a signposted junction, and downhill. When the track splits in woods (and goes right, to a house), go left. Just after the stone remains of a house on the right, go left and uphill to meet the road. Turn left and hop onto the grass verge until you come to a track going right and towards the Beacon. Turn right and clamber up to the top for some sensational 360-degree views (for more on the Beacon, see Walk 11).

From the trig point, follow the ridge downhill (south) – although the rest of the fort is well worth exploring too. At a lane turn left, then turn right, off it, at the first corner. You're now on the **Cotswold Way** and signposts should

Views from the top of Painswick Beacon

guide you easily back into the middle of Painswick from here.

In **Painswick**, when the road swings left, cross over and go down the more inviting Gloucester Road in front of you, and towards the church spire. At the main street turn right to pass the famous **churchyard** and find the car park on your left.

Painswick, mentioned in the Domesday Book, the whitest of all oolitic limestone villages, prospered from both wool and cloth with at least 25 mills in the valley. Today it's full of stylish 17th-century buildings, while the churchyard is famous for the table tombs, iron village stocks and its 99 manicured, lollipop yew trees, planted in 1792. Legend has it that every time number 100 is planted, it, or another one, dies off. Victorian poet Sydney Dobell is buried here and the church has Civil War scars from fire and canon balls. Each September there's a clipping (from the Saxon word 'ycleping') ceremony where locals join hands around the church singing hymns. Elsewhere head to Bisley Street to see 14th-century architecture and New Street for 13th-century architecture. On the outskirts of the town, you'll find the only complete Rococo Garden in England, which dates to 1720.

Old waymarker on the edge of Painswick

WALK 14
Miserden and Edgeworth

Start/Finish	Car park next to school, Miserden (SO 934 088)
Distance	7.5km (4.5 miles)
Grade	2
Time	3.5hrs
Maps	OS Landranger 163 or Explorer 179
Refreshments	Carpenters Arms, Miserden
Public transport	Buses from Stroud and (less frequently) Gloucester

A quietly beautiful and beautifully quiet walk through woods and pretty valleys in the off-the-beaten-track Cotswolds. Leave charming yet sincere hilltop Miserden to walk along a peaceful alluring valley and up to Edgeworth (which also features in Walk 19) then over the hill, through woods, to little Sudgrove and back to Miserden. A thoroughly satisfying yomp. There are some hills involved and navigation needs attention in woodlands.

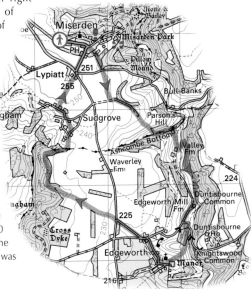

From the car park, turn right and walk to the centre of Miserden. Go to the left of the pentagonal market square-style building. Soon after, take a quick right by a public footpath sign to go between walls, then to the left of a cottage down a narrow path.

Miserden is perfectly perched on the edge of the plateau, looking down into the Golden valley and the River Frome some 240 metres below. Until the Middle Ages, Miserden was known as Greenhampstead – a name recorded in the Domesday Book. Just off route Misarden Park Gardens include a 17th-century Manor House, a whole lot of topiary and pretty flowers (open March-October; **www.misardenpark.co.uk**).

Go over a stone stile and cross a lane into a field, sticking to the wall, with tantalising glimpses of a network of secret valleys to the left, soon to be reached. In the second field turn left and downhill on a track. Ignore a left turning (despite yellow waymarker) and continue on the main track with views opening up. Where the path divides take the left downhill to a wooden stile. Continue downhill in the next field, sticking to the right to find another stile by the hedge. There's another stile soon after which takes you into trees and steeply downhill to **Ashcombe Bottom**, turning left by a fence to follow it.

Take a stile on the right to leave the trees, and turn left into a field, going past a hut and through a large wooden gate. Swing right in a pretty, remote-feeling paddock, at the bottom of the valley, towards a gate at the far end. But before the gate turn left to go over a

Heading down from Miserden towards Ashcombe Bottom

footbridge and uphill into Thick Wood, initially heading back left.

Climb for a few minutes then at a crossroad of paths turn right by a wooden waymarker. Go through a lovely stretch of woodlands and emerge in a clearing. When the trail forks continue in the same direction on a smaller path. Go through trees and downhill, and out of woods again. Follow a fence past an orchard then turn right and downhill, over a footbridge and past **Edgeworth Mill Farm**. Exit the property and go left on a lane.

Ignore the first public footpath, but take the second, just after the lane crosses the River Frome. Go between two humungous trees, over a footbridge then head right on a vague path going uphill towards Edgeworth Manor on the skyline like Dracula's Transylvanian Castle. Go through trees then follow a fence up to the impressive gate entrance of the church.

> **Edgeworth Church** dates from the 11th century and was originally a Saxon building, while the tower and porch date from the Middle Ages. The oldest piece of stained glass is thought to be a rare

Bridge over a stream just before the climb up to Edgeworth, and by two of the tallest trees you're ever likely to see

There's a stiff little climb up to Edgeworth but, as ever, it's worth it

depiction of Sir Thomas Becket and the 'Edgeworth Miracle' (the curing of a herdsman's leprosy). Grade II-listed late 17th-century (although much of it altered in the 19th century) Edgeworth Manor can be seen to the left as you leave the church. It was formerly home to German-born publisher and philanthropist Paul Hamlyn CBE.

Go through the churchyard and turn right at the lane, going uphill. The lane turns right, goes downhill then back up. At a junction turn left, then almost immediately right. At a T-junction go straight over and leave the tarmac going through a gate in front and onto a good, broad track. After a couple of fields, the track angles left, downhill into trees. At a fork, take the right, going slightly uphill. When several tracks meet, take a right, on the higher ground. Just before the track leaves the woods, veer left to go over a mossy stone stile into a field. Turn left to follow a wall towards **Sudgrove**.

Go over a stile then directly across a farm track into another field. Stick to the fence on the left to find a stile and a path by a wall. At a lane, cross over the first lane and take the lane opposite. Follow it around to the left and by two garages with faded green doors turn right and through a wooden gate into a field, keeping to the hedge on the right. You'll soon pass an inviting bench.

Go through a gate by a trig point, to a stile and a lane. Turn left, go past a blacksmith's yard and showroom. At the crossroads take the second right, back down into **Miserden**.

WALK 15
Laurie Lee's Slad Valley

[handwritten: 2/10/15 7 miles CHALLENGING GOOD]

Start/Finish	Lay-by, Bulls Cross (SO 878 088)
Distance	11km (7 miles); shorter version 7km (4.5 miles)
Grade	3
Time	5hrs; shorter version 3.5hrs
Maps	OS Landranger 162 and 163 or Explorer 179
Refreshments	The Woolpack, Slad
Public transport	Buses from Stroud, or walk from Stroud (4.5km)

'I used to think the whole world was like my valley', *Cider With Rosie* author Laurie Lee told *The Independent* in 1996. 'But I realised there was only one place like this.' He grew up in the Slad Valley in the early 20th century and it will seem delightfully familiar to anyone who's read his canonised book: 'The valley was narrow, steep, and almost entirely cut off…' he wrote, 'a jungly bird-crammed, insect-hopping sun-trap… The sides of the valley were rich in pasture and the crests heavily covered with beechwoods.' The walk passes through two nature reserves with ancient woodland. There's lots of time in trees and it's one of the most testing walks in this book.

From Bulls Cross, little more than a couple of houses and a lay-by, but where a ghostly stage-coach is said to be seen in *Cider With Rosie*, head uphill. After less than a minute turn right, by a signpost, going downhill into trees. After a gate and by a small white footpath sign, go to the right and downhill with a pond to your left. Then go steeply uphill, crossing a bigger track, on a steep climb. At a farm track with a wall turn left.

After a scrapyard behind a metal fence, turn right on tarmac. Keep to the left of the farm, swapping tarmac for a stony track. It's back on tarmac as you go downhill and as the path swings right, leave it at the corner and carry straight on with the hedge on your left.

Inside the trees the path swings left. After a tumble-down wall, go right and downhill. At the track, inch left to locate a path and carry on downhill. At the next track, repeat the same trick – straight on down. At the edge of

[handwritten: DIRECTIONS GOOD BUT STILL NEEDED TO KEEP WITS ABOUT YOU (NOT GOOD AFTER RAIN?)]

Slad has some deliciously overgrown valleys and combes, overspilling with greenery

the treeline go left slightly to a stile and the promised land: an idyllic, secluded valley.

Head downhill to the track and left to the valley's bottom. Once through a hedgerow, look uphill to the right to see a stile at the treeline. Go uphill to meet it, into the woods and steeply uphill. Look for wooden waymarking posts and at the second one, go right, through a fallen tree trunk, with a house to your left.

By a waymarker join a broader track going downhill. Ignore a yellow waymarker on a tree trunk and go straight on and to the left of a derelict house. Cross a track and go uphill. Turn right at a junction, through old gateposts and following a one-sided tree-tunnel.

The path comes out of the trees, with pleasingly overgrown undergrowth all around. The greenery soon closes in again as you enter Snows Farm Nature Reserve. ◄ Go over a stile and into an appealingly wild-looking valley. At a stile on the left, go back into the trees (too soon!).

The nature reserve is home to ancient woodland, limestone grassland flowers and a number of butterflies.

The path gradually climbs to a broader track. Turn right onto it. At a bigger track, by a house, turn left and uphill. At the tarmac turn right, to go downhill. At another house, turn right, and take the lower track to go downhill with a

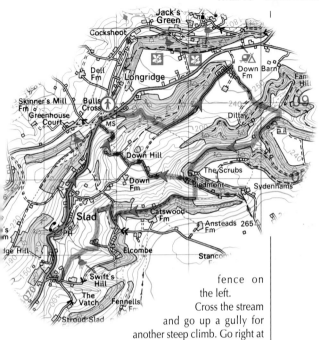

fence on the left.

Cross the stream and go up a gully for another steep climb. Go right at the top. Ignore three turnings to the left as the paths stays just inside the wood with pretty views to the right. ▶

Just after seeing a field on the left, the track doglegs right and downhill. Turn left at a junction of paths. When the path splits at a telegraph pole it doesn't matter which you take, but go left at the path just after.

Go over a stile and into fields. Stick to the top of the field with hedge on the left. Go over another stile, with lovely views right, towards Slad, although it tries to hide behind trees.

Opposite the fourth path to left, a stile on the right is the shorter route across the valley to Bulls Cross.

Laurie Lee, in his autobiographical *Cider With Rosie*, writes about his post-World War I childhood in the village of Slad. It was a time of hardship but although the book has its dark moments it's largely a tale of bucolic happiness. It sold over

The village of Slad

six million copies. Lee, also a poet, completed an autobiographical trilogy with *As I Walked Out One Midsummer Morning* (1969), about walking to Spain, and *A Moment Of War* (1991), returning for their Civil War. Lee lived much of his life in London but returned to Slad for his final years and was buried here. One of his daughters lives here and *Cider With Rosie* is still part of the English literature canon at secondary schools.

Another stile brings you to the right of farm buildings. Take the farm track, which becomes tarmaced, through Furners Farm, then leave it to the right at a stile with a yellow waymarker, downhill into trees. There's soon a stile on the right, into a pretty little field with a pond down on the left. Go over a stile and through trees, then another stile and another field. Look for a stile on the right to take you through a hedge and turn left onto a drive/track. At end of the drive, turn right on tarmac, and right again almost immediately. The road bends round to the right. Just after The Vatch house go over a stile on the right and uphill to the main road towards **Slad**. ◄ Turn

Slad was originally called Slade, meaning stream, and there were once prosperous cloth mills in the valley, although you'd never know it.

right and you'll soon find the legendary **Woolpack Inn**, Laurie Lee's former local, filled with photos of the writer, and a very tempting beer garden. Tucked behind it is Rose Cottage, where Lee lived (at least at weekends) from 1961 to 1997.

Continue up the road and after about 20 metres you pass the T-shaped Rosebank (formerly Bank Cottages), Lee's childhood home down the bank to your right after about 20 metres. Unfortunately there's a 150-metre section without a pavement so take care. A narrow pavement emerges. At a war memorial and bus stop on the right, cross the road and go left, uphill on a tarmac lane.

As the lane swings left, leave it to the right on a path that takes you into the Frith Wood Nature Reserve by a big sign: mature beech dominate, with a mix of pedunculate oak, ash and sycamore.

When you meet a bigger track, turn right. At the next junction take the higher path to the left. Cross over another track and continue in roughly the same direction. Go right at the top of the hill, which goes downhill. Ignore turnings as you leave the reserve by a sign and stick to the path, which leads you back to the road and the **Bulls Cross** lay-by.

A view across Slad Valley from (haunted?) Bulls Cross

97

WALK 16

Haresfield Beacon

Start/Finish	Shortwood car park (SO 833 086)
Distance	10km (6 miles)
Grade	1
Time	3hrs
Maps	OS Landranger 162 or Explorer 179
Refreshments	The Edgemoor Inn, Edge (just off route)
Public transport	Buses from Stroud

A short but magnificent stroll including arguably the best viewpoint of the entire Cotswold Way, from National Trust-owned Haresfield Beacon, bedecked with orchids and butterflies in summer. Elsewhere there are rewarding views of Painswick and its plump surrounding hills – worth rambling on to if there's life in those legs yet. Path-finding can be fiddly in Standish Woods (although bluebell-finding is easy in spring) but half the walk follows the Cotswold Way, making navigation easier, and there are some small hills to contend with. This is a route for those who love to wander through ancient woodland.

From the car park, fight the urge to go straight out onto Haresfield Beacon – you haven't earned that glorious view yet. Instead, go southeast through a gate (to the left as you drove in), by a Cotswold Way sign, and into the ancient **Standish Wood** (recorded in a 1297 document). Choose the middle of three paths and go downhill along a clear track. Ignore side paths for around 1km, until the path switches back left and uphill.

Follow the steep gully uphill and cross several paths, teaming up briefly with the Cotswold Way (it's confusing here but if you do go wrong aim to exit the woods near Haresfield and Stoneridge Farms) before leaving it to the right, emerging from the trees and turning right to meet a lane.

Turn left onto the road briefly and continue that way as it joins a road. Ignore the first signpost and cross the road to enter a field just after farm buildings. Go across the field angling left slightly and aiming for a white post and stile. Cross the road and go into the woods and turn right on a path.

Go through a stile on the right and cross the same road (lookout for the sharp bend). Go through a gate and after trees loosely follow the wall on the right side, down **Scottsquar Hill**. Some classic Cotswold views open up here, of Painswick and plump hills, while silver birch and their magenta branches nearer by complete a pretty picture.

The path curves left as it goes downhill. Turn left onto a broad track (or continue down to the A4173 if you want to visit the Edgemoor Inn). After a signpost on the right go left and uphill to join the **Cotswold Way** (CW) – which is now followed for the remainder of the walk.

Cross a broad track and continue uphill to cross a road and go down into woods. Ignore a path to the left and go straight downhill. At the bottom of the hill turn left onto a track. At a road turn right and follow it.

Look for an old, green CW signpost on the left near buildings and go uphill past a stone well (dating from 1870, with a witty poem inside). Pass Cromwell's Stone (a memorial commemorating the Siege of Gloucester in 1643), by yew trees.

Turn left onto a road, then a quick right to go through a gate by a barn and a stile. The path climbs steeply onto Haresfield Beacon with expansive views to the right, then chucks you out at the best spot of the walk; on **Ring Hill**, by a trig post, amid wind-battered hawthorns. Humps and mounds tell of Iron Age activity (a ten-acre hillfort, excavations found a pot of nearly 3000 Roman coins)

Along Ring Hill, a former hillfort, to some giant views across the Severn Vale

Look for kestrels and buzzards around here.

and the floor drops away to reveal big views across the Vale of Severn to the River Severn, the Forest of Dean, the Black Mountains and more. ◄

Follow the ridge back left and through a gate and by a signpost take a right down wooden steps. Turn left at the bottom and continue along the Edge, through trees and a gate, then turn right in open land to reach a topograph and more sensational views. When you're done with the vista, the **Shortwood car park** is just behind you.

WALK 17

Toadsmoor, Bisley and the Golden Valley

Start/Finish	Large lay-by on A419, 5km outside Stroud, after the left turning for Bisley and Chalford Hill and before The Pavillion restaurant (SO 877 022)
Distance	13km (8 miles); shorter version 8km (5 miles)
Grade	2
Time	4hrs; shorter version 2.5hrs
Maps	OS Landranger 162 and 163 or Explorer 168
Refreshments	Bear Inn, Bisley; King's Head, France Lynch; Lavender Bakehouse & Coffee Shop, Chalford
Public transport	Buses from Stroud

This isn't a walk that takes you away from 'civilisation' for long, but it's a joyous yomp with four distinct sections. After the ancient beech woods of clandestine Toadsmoor Valley (which has no moor and seemingly not many toads), there are fields either side of Bisley, an unheralded Cotswold beauty tucked up in trees at the head of a valley and mentioned in the Domesday Book. Take historic donkey paths down between the hill-hugging old weavers' and clothiers' cottages of steep Chalford, and then follow the abandoned Thames and Severn Canal. The route includes bits of the Wysis Way, good insight into the Golden Valley's industrial past, and the canal helps navigation. There's one long but gradual ascent and descent.

From the lay-by, head towards The Pavillion Indian restaurant and turn left uphill on the penultimate steps before it, by a house called St Kilda, on a narrow path between hedge and fence. Go left at the top, then right/uphill at a T-junction. Go left down steps by a dead end sign. Cross the road and go left then immediately right up Bourne Lane, signposted Quarhouse/Thrupp.

As the road levels out turn right, up the steep Quarhouse Lane. As road swings left go straight on taking the higher of the two lanes in front, towards Thumpers Cottage. Stay on the drive through two stone gateposts,

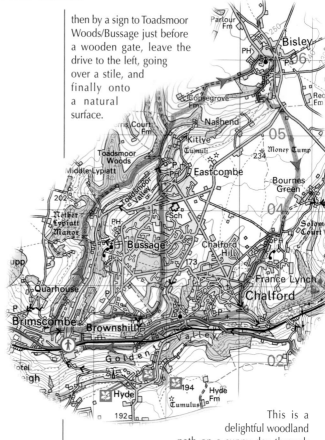

then by a sign to Toadsmoor Woods/Bussage just before a wooden gate, leave the drive to the left, going over a stile, and finally onto a natural surface.

This is a delightful woodland path on a sunny day through green beechwoods. Go over a stream and the path goes uphill. Just after the path goes downhill, go right at a fork, continuing downhill. Take a stile by a metal gate and go left and uphill. At a fork soon after, take a right. Cross another stream and take a right, sticking to the lower edge of the wood. Come out of the trees by a garage with blue doors (at the time of writing) and continue on a lane, which goes uphill to a T-junction. Turn left, downhill.

Bisley, a hidden gem if ever there was one, is tucked up at the head of a valley

Just after Toadsmoor Pond, fork right to go past the Keeper's Cottage. The path starts to go uphill, with a glimpse of a little waterfall to the right. At the top, go straight on, across another track, and onto a stony drive towards (another) Keeper's Cottage. ▶

Go to the left of the cottage and take the path that rises into the woods behind it. Ignore a path to the right, then just before a metal gate take a right to go uphill and out of the trees. Continue straight across a field looking for short wooden waymarkers.

Stick roughly to the same contour, but before a stile at the corner of a copse go left and uphill aiming – there's no definite path – to join a little-used lane with a lovely avenue. Follow it right, go over a cattle grid and turn right on another avenue, and into **Bisley**.

At the road turn left into a charming village. Go right at the first fork and right again at the next road. Just before a T-junction go right, down a lane, by Parson's Cottage, briefly joining the Wysis Way (WW). Go into the church-yard and follow the path around the **church** to a wall. Turn left and trace it downhill.

Go down steps to a lane and turn right. Follow the lane to the left. At the end of the lane turn left onto a track

If you're doing the shorter version, turn right here and make your way back along the other side of the valley, through Eastcombe, Bussage and Brownshill.

103

The Golden Valley (near Chalford) was named after the wealth created in the cloth mills here, although it could equally apply to the steep, wooded slopes

by a WW signpost. The track gets narrower, a creeper-laden tunnel of trees. At the road cross with care and go over stile to the right. Go across the middle of the field, and continue in a similar direction across fields until three hedges meet, by a singular section of fence, and you're offered two directions. Leave the WW here and go right.

Go across another field, towards Upperhill Farm. Go through a metal gate and a field, with the farm to your left. Go through another field, aiming at the farm's drive and main gate. At a lane continue in the same direction till a sign for the **King's Head** sends you left, down Lynch Road.

Keep to the right at a junction. At the next junction take the left, slightly downhill towards a phone box. After a little church ('Church Rooms') on the left, carry on downhill at a junction of five roads (as Lynch Road becomes Coppice Hill). At the next junction continue in the same direction.

When the road swings left, take a right by a grit salt box, off the road, on a tarmac path between walls. There are pretty Golden Valley views to the left as you descend.

At a junction of paths continue on. At another junction take the steps downhill to the left, then round to the right again. Continue in the same direction at the lane.

> The **Golden Valley** is a rare place where industry and natural beauty coexist happily. The name of the valley, between Chalford and Sapperton – the largest of Stroud's Five Valleys, refers to the wealth from the cloth trade using the River Frome, which once powered 150 mills. Many old mills have been converted into flats, while two continue to make felt for tennis balls and snooker tables. A labyrinthine network of donkey paths connect hill-hugging houses; Chalford was known as 'Neddyshire' (as well as 'Little Switzerland') – referencing the donkeys.

At the **A419** turn left, cross over and go past the Lavender Bakehouse & Coffee Shop, over a bridge and turn right to take the old Thames and Severn Canal towpath, which you'll be following for around 30 minutes. Look out for locks and a restored round house (used by the canal lengthman, who oversaw a particular length of water; for more on the canal see Walk 19) as you cross two roads, go under a bridge, through a tunnel and under another bridge. After a long flat section, where a river appears on the left, you'll see an old lock. Take the footbridge to the right, then cross the railway and road, both with great care, to find the **lay-by**.

Paws for thought: the France Lynch locals are a friendly bunch

105

WALK 18

*Leonard Stanley, Coaley Peak
and Selsley Common*

Start/Finish	By church, Leonard Stanley (SO 803 033)
Distance	14.5km (9 miles)
Grade	2
Time	4.5hrs
Maps	OS Landranger 162 or Explorer 168
Refreshments	Pubs in Leonard Stanley and King's Stanley (both off-route)
Public transport	Buses from Stroud

Wood-walking, field-walking and some exerting hill-walking are bookended by two of the most glorious viewpoints on the Cotswold Edge; one with a long barrow. This route stays below the escarpment for a time, building anticipation. Navigation is occasionally fiddly around fields. Some may wish to venture slightly further southwest to visit Hetty Pegler's Tump, a 17-metre Neolithic long barrow (but you'd have to walk alongside the road).

The first section, switching between fields, is a bit tricky, but if you get a bit lost, as long as you reach the Frocester Hill road you'll be back on track.

From the **church**, walk up Gipsy Lane. ◀ At a green public footpath sign turn right through a kissing-gate into a field and cross it diagonally. Go across a pair of wooden stiles, then turn right, keeping the hedge to the right. Go over a small bridge and stile and in the third field turn right across a footbridge about halfway across and left to follow the hedge again.

Near a metal farm gate, take a left and a wooden stile, then straight over another stile. The path is vague but stick to the left of the field. Go through a wooden kissing-gate by a metal farm gate and turn right. Stick to the right of the field and just after an oak tree go over a stile into a smaller field. Ignore a gate to the left and continue in the same direction to cross a stream in the trees. Turn left in the next field and follow it round to the right to a metal gate and right on a track to farm buildings.

Pass in front of a cottage and onto a lane leading downhill. Turn left on a busy road. Go through a kissing-gate at a lay-by on the right and downhill on a grassy track to the left. At a water trough by a large oak, dogleg left uphill, aiming for a house. Go over a stile near the top of the field, onto a track and past a house. Go past more houses, cross a road and kink left slightly to carry on in the same direction between hedgerows. (Where there's an option of two fields it doesn't matter which you take.)

When there's a choice between a stile and a metal gate, take the gate to go uphill. Stick to the path, ignore a bigger track, until six paths meet near a house. Take the second left (to go to the left of the **Coaley Wood** welcome sign) and uphill. Ignore paths to right then left as it gets steeper and you finally join the **Cotswold Way** (CW).

Leave the trees and turn left. Briefly take the smaller road, left and downhill, before turning back into trees on the right, and down steps. The CW emerges from the trees and stays on the Edge with some special views – which seem vast yet cosy – opening up. As well as south along the Edge and perky Cam Long Down (Walk 22), some days you can see Abergavenny's Sugar Loaf from here.

Follow the ridge through a gate behind you and through a

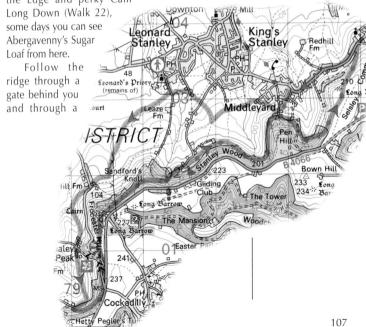

WALKING IN THE COTSWOLDS

Views towards Cam Long Down (Walk 22) from Coaley Peak

common and picnic area towards the **Nympsfield Long Barrow**.

> This **chambered tomb** dates to around 2500BC and the Neolithic period. When evacuated in 1862 the remains of at least 13 bodies (included a skeleton of a child in a stone cist or coffin) were found, plus flint arrowheads and pottery. It's typical of the Severn-Cotswold Group and the internal chambers were constructed of oolitic limestone probably quarried nearby. The long barrow has long been associated with legends and stories, including that it was a refuge for lepers.

Continue in the same direction, going back into the woods by a CW waymarker near a run-down hut on the right (which has good Long Barrow info), and not before. Go down steps and right, and continue to follow CW signposts through the wood. There are several forks, but usually good signposting (just after a kissing-gate, where the route is unclear, the two paths soon join up anyway).

Emerge in fields briefly, then back into beech trees in **Stanley Wood**. Here, follow a CW signpost going right before a farm gate. The path goes gradually uphill before undulating through a lovely section of trees (listen for jays and woodpeckers). In **Pen Wood**, just after steps, the CW splits at a signpost. Follow it straight on towards Selsley Common. Cross a tarmaced track and the hulk of **Selsley Common** comes into view. Look for a CW signpost to the right to take you steeply uphill and out of the woods. This being common land, you needn't stick to a path here.

Selsley Common hides Rabbits Burrow, Tumps Quarry and the remains of a Neolithic long barrow called The Toots. It also has remnants of a camp, established by soldiers loyal to the future King Edward I, who may have used the common as a look-out during the Baron's War (1263–1267) between King Henry III and his barons. This open grassland is also awash with wildlife. Bird's-foot trefoil, kidney vetch and ox-eye daisy are among its flowers; marbled whites and common blues its butterflies, and even common spotted and early purple orchids.

Looking out across the Severn Vale towards Wales from Selsley Common

109

The church has three large stained-glass windows made by members of the Arts and Crafts Movement, including one by William Morris.

Head vaguely right and uphill to make for the crest of the hill. Then go along the ridge, with glorious views to the left, of the River Severn and the Black Mountains. When you reach a mound/hillock at the end of the plateau your panorama doubles, with views around Stroud and surrounding valleys (including Laurie Lee's Slad, Walk 15).

Head straight downhill and you should find the CW again soon enough, turning right to let it take you towards the Selsley church. ◄ At the road turn left. Just after a long bend to the right, leave the road, on the CW, going left up a lane (or continue on, for about a kilometre, to find King Stanley's Kings Head). Then leave that to the right by a CW sign. At a lane turn right, leaving the CW, and immediately left onto a grassy track. Soon after go right and downhill by a yellow waymarker, following a fence. Turn left on a lane and head to the right of the barn. Go through the first kissing-gate (but not the second) and straight ahead into a field. At a track go left, then immediately right after a kissing-gate and over the world's smallest bridge (probably).

To find the White Hart (where 20th-century artist Sir Stanley Spencer stayed and painted during WWII), continue past the grassy triangle near the churchyard, turn right onto The Street, the pub's on the left.

After a green kissing-gate, turn left briefly on a hedge-lined path, then diagonally across a field. In the corner stay in the same field but turn to the right keeping the hedge to your left and head to the end of the field. At a lane turn right, then left after a black kissing-gate into the last field. Go directly across (ignore the path to the left) and onto Gipsy Lane, turning right to get back to the **church**. ◄

WALK 19

*Sapperton, Pinbury Park
and Edgeworth*

Start/Finish	Telephone box near church, Sapperton (SO 947 034)
Distance	11km (7 miles)
Grade	1
Time	3.5hrs
Maps	OS Landranger 163 or Explorer 179
Refreshments	The Bell at Sapperton, Sapperton; Daneway Inn, Daneway
Public transport	Buses from Cirencester (Corn Hall) and Stroud (Merrywalks)

This tasty slice of the Golden Valley includes a pretty nature reserve
(Siccaridge Wood) with rare species, plenty of history, possibly the
Cotswolds' remotest village (Edgeworth), atmospheric mossy woodlands,
views of secluded valleys and a pleasingly quiet experience. It's reasonably
well signposted, briefly includes parts of Wysis Way, and isn't particularly
hilly, although there are some short sharp gradients.

In Sapperton, park by the church
and take the path behind the telephone box, uphill between
fences. Follow the path to
the left, then downhill
into trees. Go through
a gate into a pretty
meadow, sticking to
the right. At the cor-
ner of the field, turn
left, going downhill
on a track, through
trees and a gate
and into another
meadow, aiming
at the wonderfully
located **Pinbury
Park**.

PINBURY PARK

Architect and furniture designer Ernest Gimson settled at Pinbury Park, an Elizabethan manor, with Ernest and Sidney Barnsley in the late 19th century, living there till his death in 1919 as part of a small community that was almost self-sufficient. Gimson had a furniture workshop in Daneway House, a medieval manor house in Sapperton, was a contemporary of William Morris and part of the Arts and Crafts Movement. He loved the Cotswolds, as Morris did, and today his work can be seen in the Cheltenham Art Gallery and Museum, while two Sapperton houses designed and built by the Barnsley brothers (Upper Dorvel House and Beechanger) and one designed and built by Gimson (Leasowes) survive today – near St Kenelm's Church. Poet Laureate John Masefield (1878–1967) also lived at Pinbury Manor.

The path swings right as it goes into a pretty little valley. Follow the track past a pond to a lane, turning left towards the Manor. Enter the property via a small gate but soon leave the lane to the left on a stony track, going downhill, then bending right into woods.

A very mossy tree trunk, or the feet of a green yeti?

Take a wooden footbridge over a stream, go through a gate and a stony track goes uphill in woods where

mossy tree trunks look like the furry feet of green yetis. Ignore a faint path to the left and carry on to the right to reach a gate and field. Follow the fence on the right uphill and continue through a second field towards line of six beech trees (Gloucester Beeches).

Turn right after the trees, through a gate and follow a wall, past a gate and over a stile, going downhill. Go through two gates as Edgeworth Manor and village can be seen in front. Go downhill, past a gorgeous old moss-smothered oak to find steps over a wall and into **Edgeworth**. Walk for a few minutes through the quiet village until you reach **Manor** and **church** (for more information see Walk 14). Nip through the churchyard for rewarding views across the valley.

Then retrace your steps through the village to the field. In it, take a path to the right, going uphill. Just before a telegraph pole turn left, go over a stile and uphill through trees. Then go directly across a field, to look for stile and gate to the left of the farmhouse wall. Find a stile in the hedge, by a chicken coop, to reach a lane. Turn right, then left up a track, opposite Edgeworth Polo Club.

Follow it for some time, passing a **long barrow** on the right, then go downhill, with views into pretty Far Oakridge Valley. Leave the track when it swings right and go straight ahead through a gate. In a field stick to the left to soon find a stile and go downhill with a fence on your right. After the next stile turn left, sticking to the top of the field to find a stile. Cross a footbridge then go left, uphill. Turn left on gravel driveway, on a right-of-way through private property, to reach a lane. When the lane merges with another continue in the same direction.

Turn right up steps by a sign, through private property again and quickly leave the path to cross grass and find a gate in the corner of a garden and go into big field. Go straight ahead with fence/hedge on your right, across several fields. Go over a stile, then downhill to another gate. The path bends right, downhill, with **Daneway House** in front. Go over three stiles close together. The third swings you round to the right and into a pretty plateau meadow.

Go through a gate, cross a road with care, and into Siccaridge Wood Nature Reserve.

Sapperton Valley contains rich, if small, wetlands including a chain of river meadows plus the swamps and shady pools of the abandoned Thames and Severn Canal. The ancient, coppiced Siccaridge Wood rises steeply from the wetlands and is home to many types of wildlife not found in newer woods, such as the common dormouse (now endangered), common service-tree, wood anemone and rare mountain bulin snail (*ena Montana*). Otters visit, while dippers, wagtails, water shrews and dragonflies live among the ragged robin, marsh marigold, yellow flag and purple loosestrife.

A bridge on the abandoned Thames and Severn Canal, now a wildlife haven

Follow a good path through woods. After starting to descend, at a small clearing, ignore paths to the right and left and continue on. The path gets steeper and at the bottom go over an old brick bridge. Turn immediate left to follow the canal bank, with a river on the other side.

The **Thames and Severn Canal** was built to link the Thames with the Stroudwater Canal and was part of the main thoroughfare between Bristol and London between 1789 and 1933. The deep locks and the Sapperton Tunnel were great achievements of engineering at the time but the canal faced constant difficulties, including porous limestone, and steam-powered railways meant the end of it. However, it's being slowly restored, benefiting wildlife and the wetland habitat. Old lock walls are clearly visible. And, if you're quiet, perhaps some of the wildlife too.

The last climb from the Thames and Severn Canal back up to Sapperton

Take a footbridge over an old lock and continue on the other side of canal. At the road, by the **Daneway Inn**, cross and turn right, then left after bridge, onto the Wysis Way (WW), soon rejoining the canal and woods. Go over a spooky old tunnel and into a field, angling steeply uphill towards **Sapperton**. Go through a wooden kissing-gate onto a lane and when it meets the road turn left, then right, by the church, to get back to the start.

WALK 20

*Minchinhampton and
Rodborough Commons*

Start/Finish	Weighbridge Inn, Longfords (SO 863 994)
Distance	15km (9 miles); shorter version 13km (8 miles)
Grade	2
Time	4hrs; shorter version 3.5hrs
Maps	OS Landranger 162 or Explorer 168
Refreshments	Weighbridge Inn, Longfords; Munchinhampton café, Minchinhampton; Halfway Café, Minchinhampton; The Old Lodge, Minchinhampton Common; The Amberley Inn, Amberley; The Black Horse, Amberley; Winstones Ice Cream, Bownham; The Crown Inn, Minchinhampton
Public transport	Buses to Nailsworth from Stroud (then a 20min walk)

This is a corker. It's a stiff climb up to the gloriously exposed Minchinhampton Common, which has earthworks, atmospheric woods, sensational views, wildflowers and cute little Minchinhampton. Then there's neighbouring Rodborough, with arguably even better views. From the common it's mostly flat walking. Navigation isn't a big concern as you can stroll where you please (but watch out for golf balls). With roads and dog walkers never far off it's not the quietest walk you'll ever do. But it's popular for good reason.

Park by the Weighbridge Inn and cross the road to go over the bridge opposite. Soon turn left by a cattle grid, then take a gate on the right into woods. Cross a track and carry on steeply uphill. Cross a road, into Box Wood, and continue uphill, ignoring a path to the left. After a stone stile take a left between two wooden fences, going uphill. Emerge onto tarmac and go through a metal kissing-gate and continue uphill. Cross a little green to find a path between houses. Turn left at the road and continue to a bigger road, past the Halfway Café on the right (formerly a pub). Cross the road with care and onto **Minchinhampton Common**.

Minchinhampton Common is a National Trust-owned Jurassic limestone plateau and an important archaeological landscape, with prehistoric field systems, Iron Age burial mounds, lone standing stones and the remains of a defensive earthwork known as The Bulwarks. Ancient quarries here are some of the most important Bathonian (Middle Jurassic) research sites in the UK. It's a Site of Special Scientific Interest and is known for its variety of invertebrates and butterflies (including the small blue, chalkhill blue, brown argus and small heath) and the rare Greater Horseshoe Bat (in caves towards Nailsworth). Cattle graze here in warmer months and rather enjoy causing traffic jams.

Walking through earthworks on the gloriously exposed Minchinhampton Common, towards Amberley

Start up the ditch in front of you, aiming roughly for the left of The Old Lodge (buildings among evergreen trees in middle of common), then head approximately for Amberley on the horizon. Cross a road and go through earthworks on the edge of **Amberley**. Loosely follow the houses on the left, aiming at a gap between buildings and a war memorial. Take the road to the left of the memorial. Take the next left, downhill and to the left of the Black Horse. Look for a metal kissing-gate on the right and go downhill between walls. Cross a road at the bottom and

The big and beautiful beech trees of Amberley Woods

take a track signposted 'Unsuitable for heavy goods vehicles'. As the lane meets road again, take a trail off to the right, into woods.

At a tarmac track turn left, downhill past wooden garages and back into woods. There's a confusing meeting of paths; aim to take the higher route, but the paths run concurrently so it doesn't matter greatly which you take, as long as you reach the road up Bear Hill about 15–20 minutes later.

Cross the road with care and go over a cattle grid then soon turn right (not signposted) off the lane by a lay-by of sorts and steeply uphill, out of the woods and towards a wall at the top, with gratifying views back down into the Nailsworth Valley. Near the top follow the Rodborough Common plateau around to the left to locate a couple of benches with fantastic views. ◀

For the shorter route, turn back here and head south-east to find a road that'll take you from Rodborough to Minchinhampton Common – then head for Minchinhampton itself.

National Trust-owned **Rodborough Common** enjoys even more spectacular panoramas than its neighbour, overlooking Stroud and into the deep Golden Valley on the other side. It's known for its colourful array of wildflowers and butterflies, including the pasque flower in spring and early purple orchids in May. Rodborough Fort is a folly dating from the 1760s, when a garrison of 250 men and 32 cannon protected travellers from highwaymen such as the notorious Tom Long, who was hanged nearby (there's a Tom Long's Post on Minchinhampton Common). Like Forest Green Rovers (see Walk 21), it's now owned by green energy tycoon Dale Vince.

Follow the edge of the plateau, heading roughly north, aiming vaguely for Rodborough Fort, which has old-school battlements. Swing around the fort, through trees, until you're heading back towards Minchinhampton Common. Cross the road and loosely follow it until the popular Winstones Ice Cream depot, for a well-deserved treat (the company has been family run since 1925 and have even charitably employed future guidebook authors).

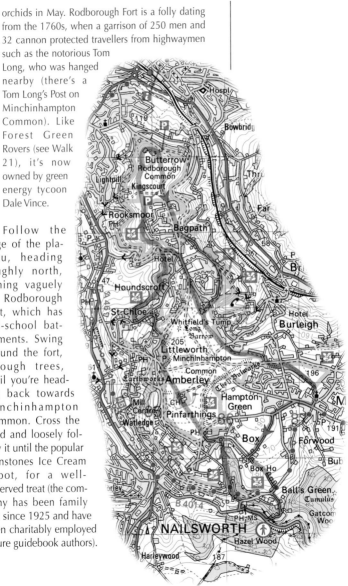

Continue downhill on the quiet road into Bownham, with views into the Golden Valley. At a fork take the right, uphill (signposted dead end). Go to the left of a couple of houses to go back onto the common, swinging left and heading towards 'Minch' again, with Burleigh on the left. Cross a road and continue in the same direction.

Meet the Cirencester road by a sign for Minchinhampton and cross with care to follow a raised path on embankment. Cross a road and continue following wall and the edge of **Minchinhampton**. When you finally run out of common, turn right, onto a lane and into the village, with a curious church on your left (the original tower was pulled down in 1863 for safety reasons).

> Handsome '**Minch**' is probably the most charming off-the-tourist-trail Cotswold village of the lot. Its pinnacle is the old-fashioned centre with its 17th-century Market House, raised on pillars, the cosy Crown Inn and pleasingly narrow, squashed-up streets – often not wide enough for cars to pass. Stone from near here was used to build the houses of Parliament and Princess Anne lives nearby.

Turn left at a T-junction to the village centre, with a war memorial and Market House building, turning right. Turn right at a road, then cross it to take a left down Cuckoo Row. Turn right at sign for Box and Hampton Green and left down peaceful Box Lane, with views across Avening Valley (see Walk 21). Go downhill into Box, then left on a footpath between walls. Take a metal kissing-gate on the left and the path descends, past a house then joins a tarmacked track.

Turn right on the **B4014**, but soon take a left, to go through renovated mills. At the main road turn right on the pavement and follow it back to the Weighbridge Inn.

WALK 21

Nailsworth and Avening

Start/Finish	Town Hall and Social Club car park, Nailsworth (ST 849 994)
Distance	10km (6 miles)
Grade	1
Time	3hrs
Maps	OS Landranger 162 or Explorer 168
Refreshments	Pubs and cafés in Nailsworth; The Bell, Avening
Public transport	Buses from Stroud

Walking from up-and-coming Nailsworth to old-school Avening (a poor man's Slad) includes plenty of woodland and some lovely views. It's wondrous in autumn. There's a convenient pub at roughly halfway and the highlight is the final descent back into 'Nelly'. The route includes parts of Macmillan Way and two fairly gradual medium-length climbs.

Not only does the small, hilly mill town of **Nailsworth** still have a town crier, but it was also home to poet WH Davies (1871-1940), aka Supertramp, who penned the brilliantly time-

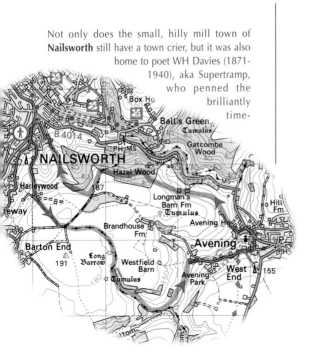

less words: 'What is this life if, full of care, we have no time to stand and stare?' He lived in four houses in 'Nelly' over the years and despite being an amputee loved walking the hills and streets. Nailsworth has a growing reputation for both culinary excellence and football. If Football Conference team Forest Green Rovers, owned by radical eco-energy tycoon Dale Vince OBE (who's banned meat from the ground – a world first – and plans to make the club fully sustainable, organic pitch and all), ever get promoted, Nailsworth will be the smallest town ever to have League football. C'mon you Rovers!

From the car park, cross over the **A46** with care, go right and slightly further uphill, then left up Tetbury Lane. At a fork with several options, continue in the same direction, past a metal gate and sign, and into a field.

Heading downhill to Avening, with good views of wooded Cotswolds slopes

Stick to the right as you follow the edge of three fields, gradually bending right and descending. Look for a yellow waymarker to go through a gap in a wall

and carry on round to the right following the wall as you descend between trees, towards a gate. Stick to the lower side of the field and trees to find another gate, with a yellow waymarker, on the right. Stick to the trees on your left to find another stile and go into woods. Follow a well-established path for some time, until you emerge into a field.

Follow trees on the left to find a gate with a waymarker. One more field, through a gate and you come to a lane. Take an immediate left. Just after a gate on the left, follow a Macmillan Way (MW) signpost into a field and head diagonally across it. According to the map, you leave the field through the copse of trees and follow the road before re-entering the field. But it's a busy road with a blind corner, so you may want to stay in the field.

From a MW signpost there's an obvious path going through the middle of the next field. Go over a stone stile and turn right to follow the wall along the field. Cross a stile, go over a lane and into the next field, with starts to descend, giving up inviting views down into the valley and towards Avening. ▶ Go over a stone stile and continue between fences.

Beech woods above Avening offer up a red-brown carpet for walkers

Like Ozleworth, Avening has a circular churchyard indicating a pre-Christian site. It also celebrates Pig Face Day every two years, a feast commemorating Queen Matilda, wife of William the Conquerer, who consecrated the church in 1080.

Leave the path by a MW signpost and turn right at the lane. Go left and downhill at a fork. At the main road, by The Bell pub, turn left, and after some new houses turn left up Woodstock Lane. Go right at the first fork, going uphill, and right at the second fork.

Leave the tarmac and go through a gate into a field, with lovely views to your right; of **Gatcombe Wood**, Princess Anne's Gatcombe House and Minchinhampton (Walk 20). It can be a riot of colour in autumn along here.

Go through a gate onto a bigger track, which goes to the left of the farm. Pass through a couple of gates by the farm and continue uphill. Go through a gate into **Hazel Wood** and take the path on the right. At a junction of paths turn left, slightly uphill, between a wall and fence. At a junction of several paths, turn right into a field by a bridleway sign, and downhill past an old stone barn. Go through a metal gate and back into the woods.

Emerge from the wood and follow a fairly obvious path down the field, with promising views of Nailsworth ahead. Towards the bottom of the field head for the bottom left corner to take a track through a gate and out onto the road.

The descent back to Nailsworth, at its best in autumn months

Continue in the same direction, past tennis courts. Turn left at a busier road, into the centre of **Nailsworth** and go left and uphill to get back to the car park.

WALK 22
Uley Bury, Dursley and Stinchcombe Hill

Start/Finish	Lay-by on B4066, Uley Bury (SO 787 993)
Distance	16km (10 miles)
Grade	3
Time	4.5hrs
Maps	OS Landranger 162 or Explorer 167
Refreshments	The Old Crown Inn, Uley (just off route); pubs and cafés in Dursley (New Inn is en route)
Public transport	Buses from Stroud

Here the Cotswold Edge curves inwards to form a crescent moon, leaving a couple of charismatic outliers guarding entry to its secluded haven. Albeit a haven – and a walk – that includes Dursley (of the Dursleys in *Harry Potter* fame – JK Rowling was born in Chipping Sodbury), but you're through it soon enough. Start by the Cotswolds' most dramatically positioned hillfort (leaving a full exploration for a climactic ending), and then follow the Cotswold Way to Stinchcombe Hill and its greedy collection of panoramic viewpoints. Then it's down through woods and a pretty arc back to Uley Bury. There's a fair bit of wood and ascent, but it's unlikely any Cotswold walk has as many viewpoints as this one.

From the lay-by, take the path downhill and to the left, joining the Cotswold Way (CW). As the ground levels out continue ahead towards perky renegade **Cam Long Down** (built by the Devil, local legend has it). At the top, follow the ridge along (curious mounds suggest at ancient earthworks and there are strip lynchets on the south-facing slopes), and soak up the rewarding views, then go down till several paths meet and turn left.

Cross a stile and a road then join a path going right, passing through fields, keeping to the right of (Victorian) Chestal House. Approaching **Dursley**, at the road turn right then left. The track ends at The Priory (heritage building). Turn left towards old Market House (built in 1738 and with a statue of Queen Anne on top). Go up

Cam Long Down was built by the Devil according to local legend

the pedestrian street, turn left at the end then right at the Old Spot pub. Go onto a track when the road swings left. Follow the path to the left, up **Stinchcombe Hill**.

At the top, head right by the golf clubhouse and follow CW markers all the way around the summit, giving you expansive views from various lookout points and benches. Until finally you come to a signpost offering the CW in three directions. Leave the National Trail here and continue in the same direction with the woods on your right. Soon join a lane with a wall on your right. When you meet another lane turn right, but go quickly left, downhill, and equally quickly turn right, off the lane into woods.

Navigation can be tricky here, but look for red paint markings and arrows. Stick to the higher path when the track divides. Stick to the higher path again near a clearing on the right. When tracks join from the left stay right as the path bends back round to the right. Just after a barrier of yellow, rusting bars and a chain turn left downhill on a track past an 'Unsuitable for motor vehicles' sign. Ignore various tracks and continue directly down when you meet a lane and again at the next junction. Turn right at the road to go past the New Inn.

The road starts to ascend. Leave it opposite a sign warning of deer, to go left on a track between hedges towards Downham Hill. ▸ When you reach a stile with a yellow waymarker, go to the right of it, uphill between hedges. Inside the trees the path continues to rise and you soon have enticing views of Uley Bury and Cam Long Down to your left. A larger track joins from the right. Take it to continue in the same direction, going uphill slightly then down. After a house go left and downhill to a lane.

Go over a stile and continue through three fields, towards Uley Bury rising in front of you, and over a road. Cross another field, turn right on a lane, then left, then right by a signpost up a steep path, and finally, you're at **Uley Bury hillfort**. It's worth walking a full circuit of the site to soak up the views and atmosphere of the dramatic position.

Known locally as 'Smallpox Hill', as it once had an isolation facility for disease victims.

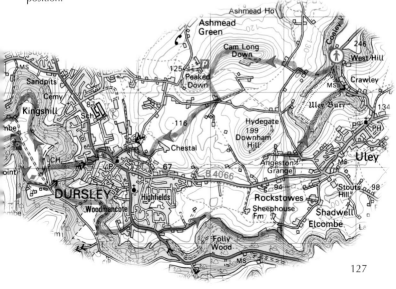

Walking along the ramparts of Uley Bury hillfort, the most dramatic in the Cotswolds

The site of Uley Bury's **Iron Age hillfort** commands magnificent views over the Severn Vale and along the Cotswold Edge, with steep drop-offs of nearly 100 metres. The boundaries of a 30-acre multi-vallate fort are easy to detect, dating from around 300BC. The site has never been excavated, but Roman coins have been found. It's the sort of place that makes you wish it were still the Iron Age so you could live here.

When you've enjoyed your explorations to the full, join the road and walk back (left) to the village.

WALK 23

Kingscote, Ozleworth and Ozleworth Bottom

Start/Finish	Just off A4135, opposite Hunters Hall pub, Kingscote (ST 815 961)
Distance	11km (7 miles)
Grade	2
Time	4hrs
Maps	OS Landranger 162 or Explorer 168
Refreshments	Hunters Hall, Kingscote
Public transport	Buses from Nailsworth and Wotton-under-Edge

Ozleworth, a curious and wonderful word, and indeed it is a wonderful and curious little-known place that feels satisfyingly wild and remote, perhaps more so than any other walk in this book. The loop includes some gorgeous green valleys, overgrown, jungly woodland and remains of Roman fortifications. There are a couple of short but stiff climbs. You'll find it hard to believe that in the 17th and 18th centuries 15 mills operated around here.

Come out of the lane and cross the **A4135** towards the **Hunters Hall pub**. Go to its left and just after a lane take a kissing-gate into a field by a sign to Newington Bagpath. Soon leave the field on an obvious track downhill into trees by a yellow waymarker.

Quickly emerge from trees and follow a grassy track through a metal farm gate and in a field stick to left. Go through another metal gate, and a wooden gate, then just after a gate by a water trough go over a footbridge. Follow the hedge to the right and uphill. At the top, cross a lane and go straight through the middle of a large arable field. By a wooden marker, bear right to follow the wall and through trees and onto Scrubbett's Lane. Turn right, ignore a left, then take a left downhill just before a crossroads and go left, off the road, and downhill through a gate into trees, with views opening up on the right.

Emerge from trees by a gate and go into delightful, tree-laden **Bagpath Valley**. Follow the wall on the left, through a wooden gate and right, downhill, between fences, and over an unusual stile-gate thing. When the fences finish continue straight downhill in the same direction. Follow occasional waymarkers to a big wooden gate and into an even prettier valley.

Go through a wooden gate by a waymarker and continue to roughly follow the valley bottom as it swings left. Stay with the stream, pass a couple of footbridges, until you reach a track. Go right, and the track swings right and uphill to quiet **Ozleworth**.

The small, enigmatic village of **Ozleworth** was listed as Osleworde in 1086's Domesday Book and before that called Oslan wyrth, meaning either 'enclosure of a man named Osla' or possibly 'enclosure frequented by blackbirds'. The churchyard is one of only two round ones in Gloucestershire (the other's in Avening), indicating it's built on a pre-Christian site. While the Saxon tower is the only six-sided one to stand in the middle of a church in the country. No two of its sides are alike, and the top storey was added by the Normans.

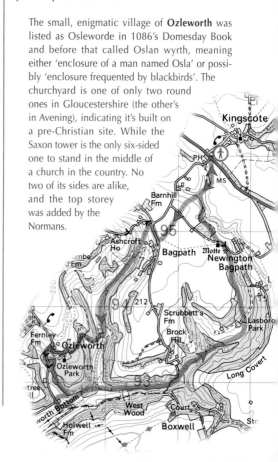

Ignore a track to the left and at tarmac go straight on. Turn right on a bridlepath by a private gate, between two hedges. At the tarmac turn right. At the next junction turn left, but not towards the big house, instead through a black gate and downhill into a field. Continue downhill on the tarmac then take a right at the junction, and stay on right at the next junction. By a house, press a button for the gate to open and go left downhill at a lane, towards **Ozleworth Bottom**.

Go left off the road just before a peach-coloured house, over a stile then right. Go across the field and turn left to trace the fence at the other end until you reach a gate taking you into woods.

Turn right on a track and cross a stream. Go through a stile and stick on the right-hand lower track. There are massive plants everywhere and it feels very jungly. Go through incongruous stone pillars and to the left of a pretty lake. After a footbridge go uphill on a track. Stick to the right of another lake and leave the woods through a big wooden gate and take a broad grassy track into pastureland.

A sun-blessed lake in Ozleworth Bottom

The path gradually swings left going uphill. Go through a gate and see old houses – one on the left and Lasborough Manor (built 1630) ahead. Cross the lane by a waymarker and continue uphill. The path's a bit vague here, but make for the top of the hill and go to the left of some fenced trees to meet a wall.

After a gate, a mound of earth and moat ahead is a 'motte', the remains of a Roman fortification. There's a disused **church** in the trees behind, too. Go to the left of the motte then downhill behind it to the corner of the field and a gate leading to a lane.

Go left and uphill, then right, off the lane, through a gate on a grassy track following a wall. Just around the corner go through a gate into the trees. Emerge from trees and continue in the same direction in a field. Stick to the right, going uphill, to find a big metal gate that will hopefully feel familiar. Then retrace your steps back to **Kingscote**.

WALK 24

Wotton-under-Edge, Wortley and North Nibley

Start/Finish	Jubilee Clock, corner of High Street and Market Street, Wotton-under-Edge (ST 757 934)
Distance	14.5km (9 miles)
Grade	3
Time	4.5hrs
Maps	OS Landranger 162 or Explorer 167
Refreshments	Pubs and cafés in Wotton-under-Edge
Public transport	Buses from Stroud (Merrywalks)
Parking	Free parking on High Street

A walk around Wotton-under-Edge, in a quiet corner of the Cotswolds. Tramp over fields to join the Cotswold Way, which takes you uphill, through woods and onto the escarpment and some big views. Then back down, up again and into more beech woods – full of wildflowers in spring and ablaze in autumn – to the Tyndale Monument on the wonderfully named Nibley Knoll (a geological Site of Special Scientific Interest) and more grand views. Cotswold Way signs help with navigation. This could easily be split into two walks.

Sleepy **Wotton-under-Edge**, tucked comfortably under the escarpment (there's a clue in the name), feels pleasingly untouched by the last few decades. However, it had its fair share of interference in the 13th century when the old market town was burnt to the ground by King John, enemy of the Berkeley Family. Rebuilt, the town did well in cloth trade of the 17th and 18th centuries. Points of interest include St Mary's Church and late 14th-century tower, Hugh Perry almshouses on Church Street, and the former Ram Inn (claims to be the oldest building in town, built 1350) on Potters Pond, which is said to be very haunted. Much-loved 20th- and 21st-century poet Ursula Askham Fanthorpe lived in the town, writing poems entitled *Wotton Walks* and *Tyndale in Darkness*.

Two ponies ponying about on the Edge above Wotton

Follow Market Street to a car park and cut across it going left heading for the right of the **church**, and down an alley. Cross a road and take the path leading to the school, then slant to the left on a wide grassy path. Go through a kissing-gate to finally escape the tentacles of town.

Go down the middle of the field towards a gap in a hedge and down the middle of the next field. Ignore a farm gate and go through a smaller one just after it, in the bottom right corner of the field. With the hedge to your left head towards **Hawpark Farm** in front of you.

After a stile near the farmhouse go left, through a gate and over a bridge. Stay to the left of two fields, heading for **Leys Farm**, and go to its left, to pass through the second gate on the right (wood not metal) and onto a track, turning left.

Cross a road, go over a stile and stick to the right/lower side of the field. Cross a stile to the right but continue in the same direction and ignore the next stile on your left but angle right here to go diagonally across the field to a stile. Cross it and go left, then through the middle of the field towards a stile and metal gate in the far corner by a road.

Cross and take a signed footpath, towards Ozleworth (Walk 23), almost opposite. Head towards a gap in the hedge in front. In the next field it doesn't matter which side of the fence you chose. Keep on in the same direction towards a stile at the field's end. In the next field, when you meet the **Cotswold Way** (CW; look for wooden waymarkers with yellow arrows) switch back left/uphill on it. Head up the field and through a kissing-gate to a lane. Cross it and follow CW signs, into woodlands on your right. Follow the steep-sided gully uphill, full of wood violets and primroses in spring and hart's-tongue in summer.

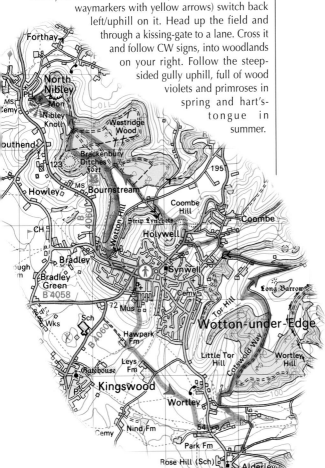

The path emerges from the canopy near the top. After half a kilometre look for a CW waymarker on your left and take the small path down steps and briefly into the woods again. Back out in the open expansive views emerge: you should be able to make out the Mendips, even the Quantocks.

Just after a drinking trough, switch right and uphill, still on the CW. The path joins a track in the same direction. Look for partridges along here, plus the hump of Blackquarries Hill **long barrow** on the right. After about half a kilometre dink left to join a lane. Stay on it for about half a kilometre with lovely views of an enticing valley to your right and strip lynchets on Coombe Hill.

As the road descends steeply in the trees look for a wooden signpost on the right, to take you down an equally steep path. Turn left at a lane, then almost immediately right. After a short distance, go through a gate on the left, just before a road junction, on a delightful path that follows a whistling stream with golden saxifrage and yellow flag in summer. Turn right onto a lane but don't take the signposted left, instead leave the CW here and continue on the lane to the B4058 and turn right. At the corner, cross with care, and go straight up a track, the leave it to right over stile into a field.

Go straight up the field, over two stiles and left by **strip lynchets** (mediaeval terraces) on steep banks above. After a spell by the side of the wood go over a stile and into trees. The path goes uphill to join a bigger track. Turn left onto it.

When the main trail bends to the right, leave it on a smaller trail to left. At a lane, cross over, angling left, and take a right, onto a stony track. Go past a gate and continue in same direction with wood on the right. Go straight on a crossroad of trails, into the woods proper.

Stay left at a junction. At a small clearing where two tracks join, ignore them and stick to the left again, on the slightly larger track. At the next clearing head straight on. At a junction by a CW sign turn right to join the trusty National Trail. Follow CW signs to finally emerge from woods as the **Tyndale Monument** comes into view sitting atop **Nibley Knoll**. ◄

Below Nibley Knoll is North Nibley, which means 'the clearing near the peak'.

The 34m **Tyndale Monument** honours William Tyndale, a North Nibley-born scholar who translated the New Testament into English. The translation challenged the hegemony of the Roman Catholic Church and English Laws. Mr Tyndale also opposed Henry VIII's divorce on the grounds that it contravened Scripture. Predictably – in retrospect – he was convicted of heresy, executed then burnt at the stake in 1536. Built in 1866, you can climb the spiral staircase of some 120 steps to the top of the tower.

From the Monument, turn left to follow the Edge back towards the wood. Then follow CW signs all the way through the wood, passing the hard-to-spot earthworks of **Brackenbury Ditches** Iron Age hillfort.

At the end of an arable field, it'd be easy to miss a wooden kissing-gate hidden slightly downhill in the corner on the right. Fantastic views open up in front of you as you go downhill to the left of the Jubilee Plantation. ▶

A walled copse initially built to commemorate victory at the Battle of Waterloo in 1815, although these aren't the original trees.

Just inside the woods, turn right and follow CW signs downhill back to Wotton. At the road turn left, then right onto a smaller road. Look for blue CW signs and soon enough you're back on the High Street.

Heading down towards Wotton-under-Edge and the Jubilee Plantation, with great views along the Edge

WALK 25

Dyrham Park and West Littleton

Start/Finish	Car park just off A46, south of M4 (ST 755 776)
Distance	9.5km (6 miles)
Grade	1
Time	3hrs
Maps	OS Landranger 172 or Explorer 155
Refreshments	Snack van (at start point on week days); Tollgate Teashop (A46, just off route); café, Dyrham Park
Public transport	Some buses from Chippenham to Bristol stop at Marshfield (then walk 4km to West Littleton)

Between Hawkesbury Upton and Cold Ashton the Cotswold Edge doesn't spoil the hiker as much as it does elsewhere (the pesky M4 doesn't help). But there's still some great walking to be had. There are gratifying views of the Severn Vale, strip lynchets and the National Trust's excellent Dyrham Park (entry fees apply; www.nationaltrust.org.uk). Wandering the Park's grounds and watching the deer could turn this into a rewarding full day's outing. If you plan to visit the Park, to avoid trudging alongside the busy A46 for a stretch, complete the walk first then drive to the Park entrance (on the A46).

From the car park, follow the slip road back out to the permanently busy **A46** and cross directly over with care. Go left a small way and right at a **Cotswold Way** (CW) signpost down a bridlepath. The path can be pleasingly overgrown in summer, with elderflowers and other wild-flowers, and poppies in nearby fields.

Out in the open, continue on, with the hedge to your right (ignore a CW signpost going left – we'll be rejoining it later). At a lane go straight over and onto a field path. It merges with a bigger path, which can be difficult to see when overgrown – look for a path going between two walls, slightly to your right.

You'll soon see **West Littleton** ahead. Turn left onto the small road and walk into the village. Turn right by the red telephone box and into the churchyard through a grey double-gate. When the path turns right to go into the **church** (parts of which date to the 13th century) head across the grass to a stone stile. Cross a horse paddock, angling right a tad to find a big gate. Then just before a wooden ladder stile, turn left to go through a little gate with a yellow marker and into an arable field.

The path isn't obvious, but stick approximately to the hedge and at the end of the first field

Just off the A46, although the Edge isn't as high along here, the views across the Severn Vale are still an absorbing spectacle

look to the side of the big hedge to get into the next field. Continue following hedges as you go through several fields and walker's gates with the ground not always predictable underfoot. The humming of the A46 never quite dies, but this is a pretty bowl of different coloured fields.

Stick to the right of a wall – and to the right of a barn – then go left before a copse and through a gate. One more field, then a lane. Turn right and cross the A46 with care and go left. ◄

The Tollgate Teashop is about 100 metres to the left.

At a large road sign for Dyrham Park look for a walkers signpost and a small metal stile. A welcome escape, and a big panorama of the Severn Vale and more. Follow the edge of the field round to the right. At a stile angle yourself diagonally left and take the track for 15 metres before turning off it to the right, by a public footpath hidden in a hedge. Keep the hedge to your left to go downhill.

As the second field swings right, take a gate to exit it steeply downhill, crossing a track. Before you get to the bottom of the field, reunite with our old friend the **Cotswold Way** by turning right, into trees.

At a lane, turn left in the pretty village of **Dyrham**. Take the first right, by a pretty little village green. You'll soon see Dyrham House, the Park's centrepiece, on your right through ornamental gates (the official entrance is at the other side).

Dyrham comes from 'deor ham' meaning deer enclosure and the herd at Dyrham Park are thought to be one of the oldest in the country. William Talman built the mansion in the 17th century, for William Blathwayt, Secretary at War during the reign of William III (seemingly, everyone was called William in those days). Dyrham Park was used as the setting for the multi-Oscar nominated 1993 film *The Remains of the Day*, starring Anthony Hopkins and Emma Thompson. As well as the grounds, there are extravagant gardens to explore, a café and child-focused fun too. **www.nationaltrust.org.uk**

Leave the road to the right by a CW signpost uphill on a wide track. When you leave the trees, pass through a couple of gates, with more rewarding views as the path bends to the right and **Hinton Hill** lies ahead and to the left.

A rose bush on the tiny village green in shady Dyrham

There was once a hillfort atop Hinton Hill and it's the site of a major Dark Ages battle in AD577 between Saxons, from Germany, and Britons/Celts. The Saxons killed three rival kings and captured Bath, Gloucester and Cirencester as a result and the victory was a major turning point in British history. There are pronounced strip lynchets (medieval farming terraces) here too.

At a lane turn left. At a bigger lane go straight over and angle left a touch to follow a path. After two long fields turn right to go uphill towards a small plantation. There are more big panoramas here – on clear days you can see the morose Black Mountains of Wales. The path bends left and around the trees before a waymarker takes you through them and back to the car park.

141

WALK 26

*Swainswick Valley
and Little Solsbury Hill*

Start/Finish	Lay-by off A46 (ST 759 685)
Distance	18.5km (11.5 miles); shorter version 11km (7 miles)
Grade	3
Time	5.5hrs; shorter version 4hrs
Maps	OS Landranger 172 or Explorer 155
Refreshments	Blathwayt pub, Lansdown Road
Public transport	From Bath bus station get any bus going east and along London Road (such as to Batheaston or Chippenham) and get off near rugby training ground seen on the right and walk up Gloucester Road

Swainswick Valley is a Cotswold Shangri-La. Just outside World Heritage-listed Bath and stuck between two busy commuter roads is a glorious natural bowl of plump pillowy meadows and slopes. It's a splendid steep valley – yet somehow peaceful and intimate – that should be overrun with walkers, yet you'll hardly see a soul. The most famous hill in pop music is nearby, and has superlative views, as is the Cotswold Edge for more vistas. This is a long, relatively challenging hike, with a lot of gradient and a couple of busy road crossings. The journey to the Edge through fields is a bit tedious (and about 3km), but worth the effort. (The shorter version cuts this out.)

From the top of the lay-by, go up steps by a green public footpath sign. Turn right at the lane, then (ignore a bridle-path) left through a kissing gate into a field, crossing it to follow a hedge uphill to the top of **Little Solsbury Hill**. Walk a circuit of the summit to soak up the views.

Little Solsbury Hill may resemble an up-turned flowerpot from distance, but it is the most famous hill in pop music. In Peter Gabriel's 1977 ditty of almost the same name the local man used poetic licence to omit the 'Little', as that doesn't sound quite so impressive when you're singing about

climbing it. Like Gabriel, the stirring views from the top may well make your heart go 'boom, boom, boom'. The sense of liberation he feels is a metaphor for his break from the band Genesis. The song also claims a sighting of an eagle, which again is either poetic licence or some serious ornithological confusion.

Views across Bath, England's most handsome city, from the top of Little Solsbury Hill, a former hillfort

Go back downhill the way you came, but turn left by a green metal signpost to follow a rough path around the width of the hill, through bushes. Soon after a public footpath sign, leave the common at a kissing-gate on the right and follow the top of the field with the fence on your left. Turn right at a lane and leave it soon, to the left, next to a wooden fence. Turn right at a fork, through a hawthorn thicket, then go left down steps and under the **A46**.

Turn right at the first junction and emerge on a lane. Go past a house with a gate but no fence (like some Monty Python sketch). Cross the road with care and go into Innox Lane and on to **Upper Swainswick**.

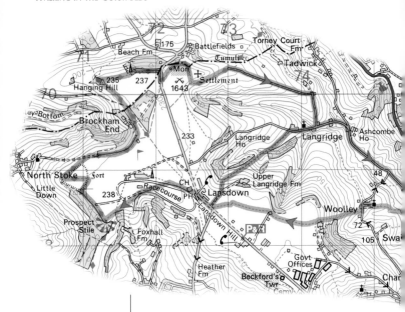

At a road junction after a school but before a church, look for a white gate on the left with a sign warning of '1 grumpy man and 2 grumpy dogs'. Tiptoe through the property and continue down a field. Go over a footbridge and stile on right, keeping the river on your left.

At the end of the field go over a footbridge sandwiched between two kissing-gates and go uphill, angling right to find a metal gate where hedge meets fence. Continue up and through a kissing-gate to a small lane between fence and wall and into **Woolley**.

Go straight on up the lane and turn left at the top of Church Street. Turn right at a yellow waymarker, onto a steep track. Turn left off it through a kissing-gate and yellow waymarker. Continue uphill sticking roughly to the right. Go past a kissing-gate and join a footpath going left and into a thicket. After a kissing-gate, there's an inviting bench with great views back. Continue climbing, go through a wooden kissing-gate and you'll finally see farm buildings ahead.

On the plateau, ignore signs to the left and carry on, angling right slightly for a stone stile. From here head northwest through a series of six fields – crossing a lane by a scrapyard, and a sports field – to finally reach a farm drive and cattle grid by Lansdown Road. ▶

Turn right, onto the pavement and cross the road after the **Blathwayt pub**. Look for signpost to go left behind the buildings. A path leads onto Bath Racecourse. Assuming there's no race on, turn right and follow white railings. When the wall on the right ends, angle left to cross racecourse (the path isn't clear but it's a right of way) aiming for trees at the other side. Turn

If you're doing the shorter version, turn right and follow a track then path back down into the valley towards Langridge.

Kelston Round Hill: a small part of the big view from Prospect Stile

145

right to follow the edge of field, finally reaching **Prospect Stile**, with massive views – including Bath, Kelston Round Hill, the Mendips and usually the Westbury White Horse.

Turn right to follow the **Cotswold Way** (CW) north, following waymarkers along the escarpment for some time, passing the Little Down Iron Age hillfort site (once 15 acres – you can still see a clear ditch). After another rewarding viewpoint, dogleg back uphill, through a golf course and onto the **Hanging Hill** trig and viewpoint. After crossing back over Lansdown Road you'll reach the **Granville Monument**. ◄

The monument commemorates a Royalist leader fatally wounded here during the Civil War's Battle of Lansdown in 1643 – the area is known as Battlefields.

Beyond the monument, look for a stile in the wall, then follow a wall and fence. At a stone stile there are long, revitalising views down into the Swainswick Valley. Go downhill just a little way to find a hedge-lined track going left – and downhill into a glorious bowl of meadows and fields. After a while you say farewell to the CW as it heads off left.

Follow the track all the way down into the valley to a T-junction and turn right. At the next junction turn left, then turn right onto peaceful Tadwick Lane, which takes you back to **Upper Swainswick**. As you come to the village green in Upper Swainswick, stay to the right to follow Tadwick Lane back out to the A46 (taking the second left), and cross it with great care (cars come fast).

Heading from Upper Swainswick towards hill-side Woolley

WALK 27
Box, Slaughterford and Colerne

Start/Finish	Market Place car park, Box (ST 826 685)
Distance	17.5km (11 miles); shorter version 10km (6 miles)
Grade	3
Time	4hrs; shorter version 2hrs
Maps	OS Landranger 173 or Explorer 156
Refreshments	Little Box Café, The Bear, The Queen's Head, Quarrymans Arms, all Box; two pubs in Colerne (just off route)
Public transport	Buses from Bath and Chippenham
Parking	At Start/Finish or Selwyn Hall car park, by the playing field (ST 824 686)

This is the perfect Byzantine valley: wide, deep, long, dotted with woodlands, mini hills, mysterious paths, curious hamlets, plus lovely viewpoints and famous little Box. The route's pretty hilly and includes parts of the Macmillan Way.

Limestone has been quarried in **Box** since the ninth century, for Bath, but also South Africa and New Zealand, but the town is more famous for its tunnel. Isambard Kingdom Brunel constructed the Bristol-London railway line in the 1830s including the world's longest underground tunnel (3.2km) at the time – through Box. It was audacious enough, but Brunel also planned for the sun to shine directly down the tunnel on his birthday, 9 April. Unfortunately atmospheric refraction meant he was two days out. Nevertheless, the tunnel entrance is still an impressive sight today (continue east on the A4 to see it). Box was also home and inspiration for Thomas the Tank Engine-author Wilbert Audrey, is home to musician Peter Gabriel, record-breaking adventurer David Hempleman-Adams, and at least one guidebook author.

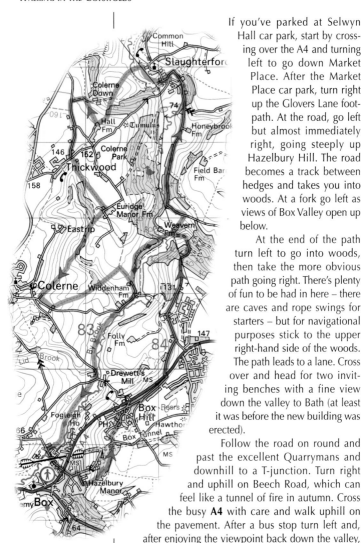

If you've parked at Selwyn Hall car park, start by crossing over the A4 and turning left to go down Market Place. After the Market Place car park, turn right up the Glovers Lane footpath. At the road, go left but almost immediately right, going steeply up Hazelbury Hill. The road becomes a track between hedges and takes you into woods. At a fork go left as views of Box Valley open up below.

At the end of the path turn left to go into woods, then take the more obvious path going right. There's plenty of fun to be had in here – there are caves and rope swings for starters – but for navigational purposes stick to the upper right-hand side of the woods. The path leads to a lane. Cross over and head for two inviting benches with a fine view down the valley to Bath (at least it was before the new building was erected).

Follow the road on round and past the excellent Quarrymans and downhill to a T-junction. Turn right and uphill on Beech Road, which can feel like a tunnel of fire in autumn. Cross the busy **A4** with care and walk uphill on the pavement. After a bus stop turn left and, after enjoying the viewpoint back down the valley, downhill on a lane.

Views back down to Box, famous for the Brunel tunnel and Thomas the Tank Engine

Follow the lane for some time. It turns into a track and goes downhill into woods. Stay to the left on the larger track and the path gets steeper and emerges from the woods. At the secretive valley bottom, cross a footbridge, turn right and uphill on a narrow path. ▸ Take a left at a bridlepath along the always-muddy Weavern Lane, enveloped in trees.

At a lane continue in the same direction, ignoring a right turn and passing the ruins of a paper mill on the left, to emerge from trees by a bridge in **Slaughterford**. Continue right, passing the bridge on your left. As the road bends right, leave it to the left, into Rag Mill Wood on a clear wide track.

Pass the Mill ruins on your right and take two footbridges over **By Brook**. Follow the river upstream on your right till you get to a gated footbridge. Angle diagonally left from here to meet a stile and go uphill between hedges. Continue through the edge of a new plantation as the ground flattens out and after a farm gate go directly up the steep hill to your left to find a path through trees to farm buildings. Turn right on a track, through the right of two farm gates, and downhill sticking to the higher track.

Or, if you are doing the shorter version, after the footbridge turn left and follow the Macmillan Way back into Box.

Turn left to go uphill, to a lane and turn left. Take the right at a junction and you soon meet a bigger lane in **Thickwood**.

Cross over a lane and go through a gate into the field opposite, signed Euridge, on a track at first then following the contour round to the right and behind trees. Continue in the same direction through two more fields to farm buildings and a lane. Turn right but leave the tarmac almost straight away over another stile in front of you and down a steep field, angling for the bottom right corner. Look for a stile hidden in the hedge before the bottom of the slope.

Turn left on a track going downhill. When you meet a metal gate, take a stile to the right, uphill, then left and into a tunnel of trees, still going uphill. Follow this to a lane.

Turn left and downhill (or right, to visit **Colerne**, which has two pubs). By a barn go over a stile on the left into a long field and down its middle. In the next field stick loosely to the left to find a footbridge. In the next field angle diagonally right and uphill to go through a

Following By Brook past willow trees and along the Macmillan Way back into Box

clump of trees and into another field on flatter ground. Stay to the right and at a gate turn right, into another field, sticking to the hedge on the left, going downhill. After a barn, take a narrow, steep but short path to the left. At the lane turn right. After a farm, leave the lane to the left and into a field. You're back on the **Macmillan Way**.

Climbing out of Box on a tree-cloaked lane can be a joy in summer

Follow the river along to another stile by another farm and turn left at the lane. At a fork turn right. Soon take a kissing-gate on the left, into a short field to another kissing-gate and into a bigger field. From here follow the river through two pretty fields, past some poetic weeping willows and plenty of bird life centred on the pea green water.

Stick by the river to find a stile and path that goes through trees and over two footbridges to a lane. Turn left and go under a railway tunnel to find the **A4** and the centre of **Box**, opposite Market Place. If you're thirsty or peckish, the Post Office shop and a café are five seconds to your left and there are two pubs just two minutes along the road to the right.

WALK 28
Saltford, North Stoke, Weston

Start/Finish	Lay-by near Bird in Hand (pub), Saltford (ST 689 675)
Distance	15km (9 miles); shorter version 9.5km (6 miles)
Grade	3
Time	4.5hrs; shorter version 2.5hrs
Maps	OS Landranger 172 or Explorer 155
Refreshments	Bird in Hand, Saltford; The Swan, Swineford; The Boathouse, Newbridge; The Riverside, Saltford
Public transport	Buses from Bath city centre
Parking	If the above is full, go south along the river about half a mile to find a larger parking area

Ever wondered what it's like walking those final few miles of the Cotswold Way down to Bath? Well this is the cheat's way to find out. This route includes the fittingly spectacular grand finale of a long slope descent with some outstanding views. But before that you've a hearty ascent and afterwards lots of riverside strolling. As it uses parts of the Cotswold Way and the River Avon Trail navigation is mostly straightforward.

Walk uphill from the lay-by to the Bird in Hand (pub) car park and turn left, up steps to the **Bath Railway Path**. Turn left and follow it for about 2km.

After a bridge, turn left off the lane and downhill, then another left to go under the bridge and simply follow the **River Avon** through fields into **Swineford**, with appetising views of Kelston Round Hill and the Cotswold Edge in front.

At the **A431** in Swineford, cross with care and go to the right of **The Swan** (pub) up a lane and through a couple of gates and a farmyard, aiming for the left of a barn (don't let a lack of public footpath signs put you off). Then ahead on a lane, past a picnic site sign. Turn right, just before a car park, to a stile. Go directly across a field, and the next, as they get steeper. Then up a steep wooded gully.

The path swings left and levels out a bit, then swings right and mutates into a track. At the lane turn left and head uphill towards the church. Go to the left of it and take a right, just after it, into a field, and round the back of it.

Head steeply uphill with big views opening up behind, of Bristol, the Mendips and more. Go over a stile and carry on up even more steeply past a wooden way-marker. Go to the right of a fence, joining the **Cotswold Way** (CW) as you do, to go through a kissing-gate and reach the plateau.

Go straight across the field then swing right by a wall – and the site of an Iron Age **hillfort**. Follow the Edge to **Prospect Stile** where there's a topograph and a vast pano-rama, including Bath, the Mendips, the Westbury White Horse gleaming on a hillside and tree-topped Kelston Round Hill just in front.

Continue on the Cotswold Way, gradually down-hill, following regular waymarkers, all the way down to Weston (Bath suburb). ▸

Shortcut

To return to the start from Prospect Stile, set off downhill on the CW then take a right, then a left, down through Kelston and back to the start.

Views up towards Kelston Round Hill on the way to Swineford, walking alongside the River Avon

There's a chance to detour to the summit of Kelston Round Hill as you descend.

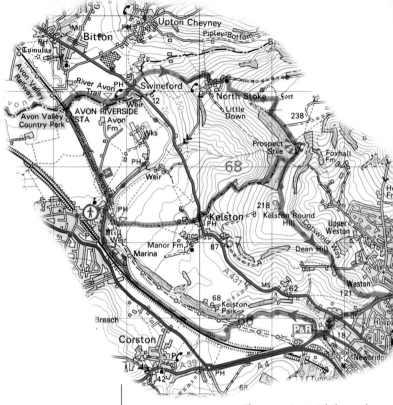

The route is straightforward as you gradually descend, briefly on a lane before hopping back into the green and brown stuff via a stile. After a trig point on the right the path steepens and when you reach a flat field with goalposts, leave it at the far-right corner and bid farewell to the Cotswold Way.

Turn right and follow the road back the way you've just come, crossing over when the pavement runs out. After a large garage behind a gate on the right, cross the road and take the slip road with a high hedge. Then in the same direction, go down a footpath between wall and hedge. At the road turn right and cross over. Go down steps on the left, through a metal gate and downhill on a narrow path.

Back out in the open, head left at a lane, then right, down a path before a car park. At the Boathouse (pub) head towards the bridge and take the steps up to meet the road. Turn right, cross the bridge, then right again and back down to join the River Avon Trail, which will take you all the way back to Saltford – some 30 minutes away at least.

The **River Avon Valley** cut its way through the Cotswold escarpment during the Ice Ages of the last million years. Fossils of woolly mammoth teeth and tusks have been found near the river, as have Stone Age flint tools. Many thousands of tonnes of Bath Stone were carried by boat down the Avon, some exported to America and South Africa.

Not long after some boat sheds and a footbridge, at The Riverside pub, follow the drive out to the lane, turn right and continue on, past the Saltford Brass Mill (a scheduled ancient monument), finally reaching the **Bird in Hand pub** again.

Barges on the River Avon at the edge of Bath – following the river makes for easy navigation

WALK 29

Bath Skyline

Start/Finish	The Avenue, near Bath Cats and Dogs Home (ST 779 642)
Distance	9.5km (6 miles)
Grade	1
Time	3hrs
Maps	OS Landranger 172 or Explorer 155
Refreshments	Pubs and cafés in Bath (but none en route)
Public transport	City Sightseeing bus from Bath Spa station, alight American Museum, or buses from City Centre to Bath University. The walk is a mile from Bath city centre.

Walks near cities that make you feel nowhere near a city are to be treasured. But when urban views are unavoidable, there's not a more handsome city in England than World Heritage-listed Bath. The Georgian city's tasteful terraces and bountiful syrupy goodness sit in a natural bowl of seven hills, rather like Rome, and this stroll offers gorgeous views of it (well, if you ignore the ugly giant gasometer), plus wild flower-dotted meadows, quiet woods, little hidden valleys and a fake castle. It's very well signposted (look for circular white markers), with a few short sharp hills. Look for wild cowslip and knapweed – which attracts the black and white wings of the marbled white butterfly.

From The Avenue, walk about 100 metres (east) down the road till you see a white, circular Bath Skyline way-marker to your left on a style. Go through the wall and after about 20 metres turn right at a fork, go through gate, then left onto a track. Follow the path to the corner of the field, then go through a gate and left across a field. At a corner, go through a gate and across another field, with woods on your right. At end of the field go through gate into Bathampton Woods.

At a fork bear right and keep to the main trail. Leave the woods and continue straight on, with big views into Wiltshire opening up – and of Little Solsbury Hill (Walk 26) of Peter Gabriel fame. Bear left, slightly uphill,

heading towards the right of the TV masts. The path gradually moves away from the woodland on the right and joins a track to the right of masts.

The National Trust-owned Bath Skyline walk is the best waymarked route in this guidebook

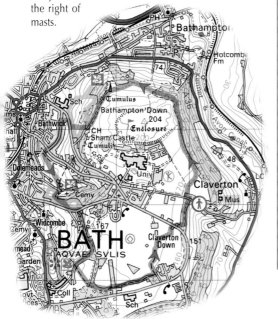

157

From here there's a short, recommended detour uphill to Sham Castle, an 18th-century folly commissioned by Ralph Allen, Bath's postmaster.

Follow the track to the second gate on the right, and down into woods. The path drops steeply. Go left just before a fence. Continue through the trees and up wooden steps to a bench with a great viewpoint. ◄

Return to the route and go through a gate on the right of stone pillars and downhill. At the bottom of the slope go through a gate onto a road and turn right along the pavement. Take a footpath left and downhill to Clevedon Walk (road), then turn left. Standing on **Bathwick Hill**, with your back to Cleveland Walk, take the path opposite that goes between houses.

Go through a gate and bear left diagonally across a field. Go through two gates and through Richens Orchard. Cross a track to a gate and uphill. Bear diagonally left uphill across a field towards houses. At the far corner turn right after a gate, to a road, then left and uphill. After the last house on the right, cross the road and go uphill through woods.

Sham Castle: built by a chap who, not unreasonably, wanted to see a castle from his window

At a gate turn right and go straight ahead to a gap in a wall. After about 100 metres across a field take the path bearing right, away from a gravel track. Enter trees, cross

a junction of tracks and follow steps downhill. At the bottom turn left before a gate.

At a gateway turn left and uphill through trees to playing fields, then turn right, keeping the fence on the left. Go through a gate onto a track, then through another gate into woods. Cross a private drive and go straight on through woods. Follow a path to the right as it skirts an old quarry and arrives at houses at the woods' edge.

Turn left into a field. Keep the boundary on your right and at the end of the field take the right of two gates and follow a path by a wall. At the main road turn left, then right, down a narrow footpath. Go straight on at a playing field, keeping the boundary immediately on your left and come to Bath Cats and Dogs Home (you can usually hear it before you see it) and the Avenue.

Views go right across the city to Kelston Round Hill, Bath's signature hill, on the distant horizon

WALK 30

Bradford-on-Avon and Farleigh Hungerford Castle

Start/Finish	Train station car park, Bradford-on-Avon (ST 825 606)
Distance	14.5km (9 miles)
Grade	2
Time	4hrs
Maps	OS Landranger 172 and 173 or Explorer 156
Refreshments	Pubs and cafés in Bradford-on-Avon; Stowford Manor Farm, A366; The Inn, Freshford; Cross Guns, Avoncliff
Public transport	Trains and buses from Bath

Although the Cotswold Way ends at Bath, the Cotswold Area of Outstanding Natural Beauty doesn't. Strictly speaking, Bradford-on-Avon is just outside the designated area, but the northwest part of this route, around Freshford, passes through it and this area is well worth a visit. This walk will give glee to river and canal admirers, has more history than seems fair and some of the finest, long lazy valley-strolling the country has to offer. Waterways aid navigation and the only fiddly bits are through villages and fields. There is one short sharp ascent and one gradual descent. Includes parts of the Macmillan Way.

Take a left out of the train station car park and left again into the war memorial gardens just before the bridge. Reach the River Avon and turn left. Leave it briefly, going through a wall, to the left of St Margaret's Hall (not over the bridge) and to the right of the Riverside Inn to rejoin the paved, riverside path, soon leaving the town behind.

Wiltshire's **Bradford-on-Avon**, set in a wooded valley with syrupy limestone terraces, is something of a mini Bath. The settlement dates back to the Iron Age and the town's name comes from 'broad ford' – now a 13th-century bridge. The town was a prosperous centre of the wool and cloth trade and the much-prized church is Saxon (13th century). Alternative and healthy lifestyles are well represented here and there are plenty of fine cafés and interesting shops about.

Go under a railway bridge, ignore a left turning and turn right when the path meets a lane, passing the 14th-century **tithe barn** on your left. Stick to the riverside and after about half a kilometre follow the tarmac lane as it swings left, to the Kennet and Avon Canal.

Take the wooden footbridge over the canal and turn right. After a smaller footbridge and kissing-gate stick to the canal-side of the field. In the next field turn sharp left to go steeply uphill to a stile, with views back to Bradford-on-Avon. Go directly across the next field, uphill to a wooden stile. After another wooden stile go over a stone stile and follow a path between hedges and through private property, to a lane. Cross it and go into fields. Head diagonally across the field to a gap in the

Following the Kennet and Avon Canal is peaceful and makes navigation easy

The similarly-aged, National Trust-owned Westwood Manor is on the other side of the church; **www. nationaltrust.org.uk**

hedge and two stiles – take the right. Stick roughly to the left through fields to reach **Westwood**.

At a lane continue in the same direction to a T-junction. Go straight over, up steps and along an alleyway. At a junction of tracks by a wall corner turn left towards the 15th-century **church**. Go to the right of it, through the churchyard and to a lane. ◀

Cross the lane and go over a stile on the right. Stick to the left in a field to pass a tree-ringed pond, and go across the next field to a wooden stile in a hedge. The next field starts to go downhill. Find a wooden stile by a metal gate and go down the next field. Follow the natural curve of the land round to the right, to a gap in the hedge. Then angle left to cross the corner of a field. Cross a stream as you go right, into the world's tiniest field (possibly). Then through a gate and into the last field. Keep to the right/the stream to reach farm buildings and the **A366**.

Turn right and cross the road to take the second left by a brown sign for **Stowford Manor Farm** (which has a café, B&B and craft workshops). Just inside the property, turn right to head across fields, following the River Frome until you reach a road, not long after seeing Farleigh

Hungerford Castle on the horizon. Cross the road and turn left to cross the bridge – with great care. Find a pavement after the second bridge and follow the road to the **Castle**.

> The 14th-century fortified mansion of **Farleigh Hungerford Castle** was occupied for 300 years by the Hungerford family, whose stories, some of which would be too outlandish for a soap opera, are told through interpretation panels and a free audio tour. The chapel has rare medieval wall paintings, family tombs and the best collection of human-shaped lead coffins in Britain. Entry fees apply. **www.english-heritage.org.uk**

Just before the Castle entrance, go down steep steps to the right. Meet a lane and continue in the same direction (joining the **Macmillan Way**), then go right just after a tiny bridge, to follow the River Frome again. From here you're following the river until it meets the Avon, then following that and the canal back to Bradford-on-Avon.

Medieval Iford Manor and a 600-year-old bridge, just off-route

At a lane, turn right for a brief detour to see the handsome, medieval Iford Manor (opening times limited; **www. Ifordmanor.co.uk**) and the 600-year-old bridge in front of it.

Go left over an amusingly well-signposted footbridge, through a kissing-gate into a pretty valley, which is home to rare species including kingfishers, otters, water voles, greater horseshoe bats and egrets. ◄

Turning back, go right, into a field, opposite where you entered the lane and continue on in the enchanting valley. Look out for a gate and stile on the left to take you reluctantly uphill slightly through a wood. Leave the woods and, at a lane, turn left and almost straight away right, go over a footbridge and uphill. Go through a wooden gate and onto a bridleway.

At a lane in front of 18th-century Dunkirk Mill Cottage turn right and follow it downhill to a bridge. Instead of going over it, continue on, through a wooden kissing-gate. After a couple more gates the path climbs to **Freshford**. Here, go right through a metal kissing-gate and – hilariously – all the way back down. Before you reach **The Inn**, cross the River Frome on a triple-arched bridge. Then turn left into a field to follow the slaloming water.

By a railway bridge swap the River Frome for the River Avon and go through Tess' Gate (surely the prettiest such thing in the Cotswolds) into another pleasant valley, replete with cherry blossoms. Sadly, the path jumps up the bank.

Go under the bridge at **Avoncliff**, uphill to the right of the **Cross Guns pub** and turn left to follow the canal towpath. Reaching the footbridge over the canal you used earlier, you can choose between the familiar route and following the canal back to town.

APPENDIX A
Route summary table

Walk	Start/Finish	Distance	Grade	Time	Page
1	Chipping Campden	18km (11 miles)	2	5hrs	27
2	Overbury	15km (9 miles)	3	4hrs	33
3	Stanton	13km (8 miles)	2	5hrs	38
4	Long Compton	14km (9 miles)	2	4.5hrs	43
5	Winchcombe	19km (12 miles)	3	6hrs	47
6	Winchcombe	12.5km (8 miles)	2	3.5hrs	52
7	Temple Guiting	11.5km (7 miles)	1	3hrs	57
8	Bourton-on-the-Water	16km (10 miles)	2	5hrs	61
9	Near Seven Springs	16.5km (10 miles)	3	5hrs	66
10	Chedworth	13km (8 miles)	2	4hrs	71
11	Cranham	11km (7 miles)	2	4hrs	76
12	Brimpsfield	9km (5.5 miles)	2	3.5hrs	82
13	Painswick	12km (7.5 miles)	2	4hrs	85
14	Miserden	7.5km (4.5 miles)	2	3.5hrs	89
15	Bulls Cross	11km (7 miles)	3	5hrs	93
16	Haresfield Beacon	10km (6 miles)	1	3hrs	98

Walk	Start/Finish	Distance	Grade	Time	Page
17	A419, near Stroud	13km (8 miles)	2	4hrs	101
18	Leonard Stanley	14.5km (9 miles)	2	4.5hrs	106
19	Sapperton	11km (7 miles)	1	3.5hrs	111
20	Longfords	15km (9 miles)	2	4hrs	116
21	Nailsworth	10km (6 miles)	1	3hrs	121
22	Uley Bury	16km (10 miles)	3	4.5hrs	125
23	Kingscote	11km (7 miles)	2	4hrs	129
24	Wotton-under-Edge	14.5km (9 miles)	3	4.5hrs	133
25	Just off the A46, south of Dodington Ash and the M4	9.5km (6 miles)	1	3hrs	138
26	Swainswick	18.5km (11.5 miles)	3	5.5hrs	142
27	Box	17.5km (11 miles)	3	4hrs	147
28	Saltford	15km (9 miles)	3	4.5hrs	152
29	The Avenue, near Bath	9.5km (6 miles)	1	3hrs	156
30	Bradford-on-Avon	14.5km (9 miles)	2	4hrs	160

APPENDIX B
Long- and medium-distance walks in the Cotswolds

The Cotswolds Area of Outstanding Natural Beauty is crisscrossed by a staggering number of long- and medium-distance paths, many briefly tiptoed upon in this book. Here are the better-known ones.

The Cotswold Way
This brilliant National Trail hugs the escarpment for 164km (102 miles), from Chipping Campden to Bath and it just so happens Cicerone has a guidebook for it. www.nationaltrail.co.uk

The d'Arcy Dalton Way
The 107km (66-mile) route links the Oxford Canal Walk, Oxfordshire Way, Thames Path and Ridgeway. www.ldwa.org.uk

The Gloucestershire Way
From Chepstow, this 151km (94-mile) route climbs the escarpment then hops across the hills to Salperton, Stow-on-the-Wold and Winchcombe, then back to Tewkesbury. www.ldwa.org.uk

The Diamond Way
A roughly diamond shaped 105km (65-mile) trail starts at Moreton-in-Marsh and goes to Guiting Power, near Bourton-on-the-Water, and Northleach. www.ldwa.org.uk

The Gustav Holst Way
A 55km (34-mile) trail from Cranham to Wyck Rissington, calls at places connected to the Cheltenham-born composer who wrote *Cotswolds Symphony*, a musical eulogy to the region. www.holstmuseum.org.uk

The Heart of England Way
The 163km (101-mile) route runs from Cannock Chase AONB, Staffordshire to Bourton-on-the-Water. www.heartofenglandway.org

The Limestone Link
A route of 58km (36 miles) joins the limestone hills of the Cotswolds (and the Cotswold Way) to the similarly created Mendips (and the West Mendip Way). www.ldwa.org.uk

The Macmillan Way
The main Macmillan Way runs 461km (287 miles) from the Lincolnshire coast to the Dorset coast and includes the 138km (86-mile) Cross Cotswold Pathway, from Banbury to Bath; and a Cotswold Link, from Chipping Campden to Banbury. Use the Cotswold Way to complete a massive 'Cotswold Round'. www.macmillanway.org

The Monarch's Way
A 990km (615-mile) trail from Worcester to Shoreham-by-Sea in Sussex that roughly follows the escape route of King Charles II in 1651 after defeat at the Battle of Worcester.

The North Cotswold Diamond Way
A 96-km (60-mile) circular tour of the North Cotswolds, linking Ebrington, Oddington, Northleach and Guiting Power. www.ldwa.org.uk

The Oxfordshire Way
This 108km (67-mile) trail between Bourton-on-the-Water and Henley-on-Thames links the Heart of England Way with the Thames Path National Trail. www.oxfordshire.gov.uk

The Palladian Way
Named after the classical style of architecture, the 190km (118-mile) trail connects Buckingham's Old Gaol with Bath's Pulteney Bridge, via classical houses and estates. www.ldwa.org.uk

The River Avon Trail
A 37km (23-mile) trail from Pill in North Somerset to Pulteney Bridge, Bath. www.riveravontrail.org.uk

St Kenelm's Way
A 80km (50-mile) trail from Worcestershire's Clent Hills, the scene of St Kenelm's murder, to Winchcombe and his final place. www.countryside-matters.co.uk

The Thames Path National Trail
The Cotswold's other National Trail follows the river for 294km (184 miles) from its source near Cirencester to the Thames Barrier, Greenwich.

The Warden's Way and the Windrush Way
Two 22km (14-mile) links between the Oxfordshire Way at Bourton-on-the-Water and the Cotswold Way at Winchcombe. The Windrush takes to the hills, while the Warden's goes through the Slaughters, Naunton and Guiting Power. www.ldwa.org.uk

The Winchcombe Way
A figure-eight 68km (42-mile) trail created by the excellent folk of Winchcombe to showcase the bets of the north Cotswolds. www.winchcombewelcomeswalkers.com

The Wychavon Way
This 67km (42-mile) route links the River Severn and the Cotswolds through the Vale of Evesham. www.worcestershire.gov.uk

The Wysis Way
A 88km (55-mile) route that links the rivers Wye, Severn and Thames, from Monmouth to Thameshead. www.countryside-matters.co.uk

APPENDIX C
Bibliography and further reading

Bingham, Jane, *The Cotswolds: A cultural history* (Signal Books, 2009)

Bryson, Bill, *Notes From A Small Island* (Random House, 1995)

Copeland, Tim, *The Cotswold Way: An archaeological walking guide* (The History Press, 2013)

Gissing, Algernon, *The Footpath Way in North Gloucestershire* (The History Press, 1924)

Gooley, Tristan, *The Natural Explorer* (Sceptre, 2012)

Gooley, Tristan, *The Natural Navigator* (Virgin Books, 2010)

Grove, Valerie, *Laurie Lee: The Well-Loved Stranger* (Viking, 1999)

Hall, Ken and Govett, John, *Where to Watch Birds in Somerset, Gloucestershire and Wiltshire* (Christopher Helm, 2003)

Hill, Susan, *The Spirit of the Cotswolds* (Mermaid Books, 1988)

Lee, Laurie, *Cider with Rosie* (Vintage Classics, 1959)

McCarthy, Fiona, *William Morris: A Life for our time* (Faber and Faber, 2010)

Nanson, Anthony, *Gloucestershire Folk Tales* (The History Press, 2012)

Priestley, JB, *English Journey* (Victor Gollancz, 1934)

Reynolds, Kev, *The Cotswold Way* (Cicerone Press, 2007)

Sterry, Paul, *Collins Complete Guide to British Wildlife* (Collins, 1997)

Talbot, Robert, *Winchcombe Way: The official guide* (North Cotswold Walkers, 2011)

Teller, Matthew, *The Rough Guide to the Cotswolds* (Rough Guides, 2011)

Williams, Isobel, *With Scott in the Antarctic: Edward Wilson: Explorer, naturalist, artist* (The History Press, 2009)

APPENDIX D

Websites and further information

Heritage and conservation
Cotswold Canals Trust
www.cotswoldcanals.com

English Heritage
www.english-heritage.org.uk

National Trust
www.nationaltrust.org.uk

The Cotswolds Conservation Board, the Cotswold Voluntary Wardens and for events
and activity information:
www.cotswoldsaonb.org.uk

Tourist information

Official Tourism website
www.cotswolds.com
for what's on, things to see and do, and accommodation options.

Tourist information offices
Bourton-on-the-Water
Tel 01451 820211
bourtonvic@btconnect.com

Cheltenham
Tel 01242 522878
info@cheltenham.gov.uk

Chipping Campden
Tel 01386 841206
info@campdenonline.org

Cirencester
Tel 01285 654180
cirencestervic@cotswold.gov.uk

Gloucester
Tel 01452 396572
tourism@gloucester.gov.uk

Stroud
Tel 01453 760960
tic@stroud.gov.uk

Tetbury
Tel 01666 503552
tourism@tetbury.org

Winchcombe
Tel 01242 602925 (Saturdays and Sundays only in winter)
winchcombetic@tewkesbury.gov.uk

Travel and orientation
AA Route Finder (for planning car journeys)
www.theaa.com/route-planner

Ordnance Survey
www.ordnancesurvey.co.uk

For public transport
www.transportdirect.info
http://traveline.info

Walking groups and related sites
Gloucestershire Ramblers
www.gloucestershirearearamblers.org.uk

Long Distance Walkers Association
www.ldwa.org.uk

Ramblers
www.ramblers.co.uk

South Cotswold Ramblers
www.southcotswoldramblers.org.uk

The Cotswold Way National Trail
www.nationaltrail.co.uk/cotswold

Wildlife
Gloucestershire Wildlife Trust
www.gloucestershirewildlifetrust.co.uk

Natural England
www.naturalengland.org.uk

Royal Society for the Protection of Birds
www.rspb.org.uk

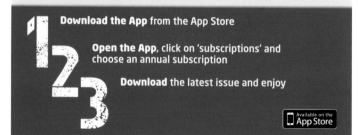

LISTING OF CICERONE GUIDES